The European
STATES SYSTEM

A Study
of International Relations

By

R. B. MOWAT

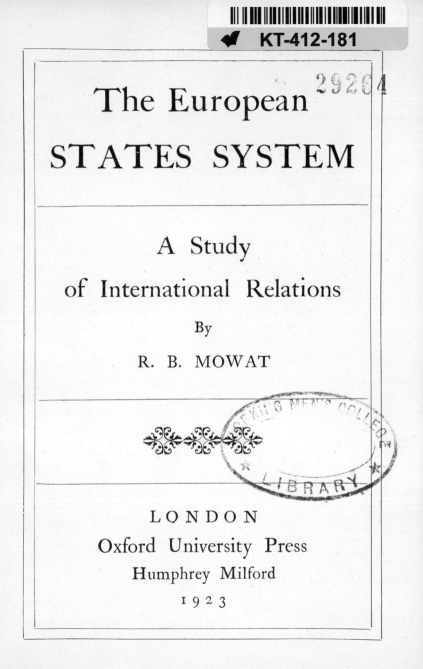

LONDON

Oxford University Press

Humphrey Milford

1923

Oxford University Press

London   Edinburgh   Glasgow   Copenhagen
New York   Toronto   Melbourne   Cape Town
Bombay   Calcutta   Madras   Shanghai
Humphrey Milford Publisher to the UNIVERSITY

Printed in England

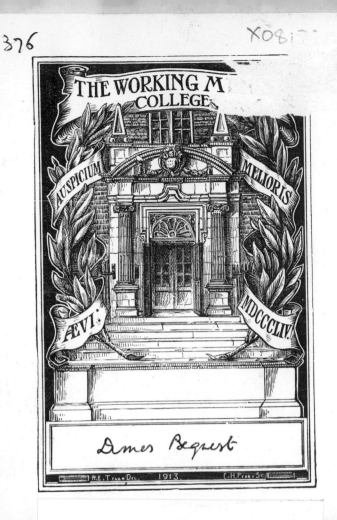

THE WORKING M COLLEGE

AUSPICIUM MELIORIS

ÆVI: MDCCCLIV.

Ames Bequest

R.E.Tyler.Del. 1913. C.H.Perry.Sc.

WORKING MEN'S COLLEGE

LIBRARY REGULATIONS

The Library is open every week-day evening (except Saturday), from 6.30 to 10 o'clock.

This book may be kept for three weeks. If not returned within that period, the borrower will be liable to a fine of one penny per week.

If lost or damaged, the borrower will be required to make good such loss or damage.

Only one book may be borrowed at a time.

CONTENTS

I

THE EUROPEAN SYSTEM

II

THE SYSTEM FOUNDED AND CHALLENGED

III

LOUIS XIV

IV

THE SYSTEM TESTED

V

THE REVOLUTION

VI

THE CONCERT OF EUROPE, 1815–56

VII

VIII

THE EUROPEAN SYSTEM, 1870–1914

I

The European System

§ 1

'THE history of the Political System of Europe', says Heeren (*History of the Political System of Europe and its Colonies,* Introduction), 'must not be confounded with the history of the separate States of which it is composed.' Each State has a life of its own, and its citizens live together and form one society; but the States of Europe have to live together too, and they likewise form one society. And just as inside the State people must behave towards each other with honesty and courtesy, so between States there are recognized modes of conduct. 'Good manners', a definitely known although not explicitly formulated code, regulate individual relations; so does diplomacy or 'diplomatic practice' regulate international relations.

Inside the State, the rules of good behaviour are enforced by public opinion and have the strength of ancient customs. But behind public opinion and custom are the laws of the land, which ultimately enforce the elementary rules of conduct, 'thou shalt not kill, thou shalt not steal'; and these laws are obeyed, partly because the citizens desire to obey them, and partly because the physical force of the State causes them to be obeyed. Law—municipal law, the law inside the State—is 'the armed conscience of the community'.

So, too, to regulate the relations between States there is a positive law. Diplomacy, the recognized mode of conduct between the officials of different States, regulates normal international relations. But more specific regulations are necessary to define the attitude of particular States to each other, to adjust

their present or future behaviour. These particular regulations
are contained in treaties. And just as ordinary laws inside the
State are observed, partly because we think it right to observe
them, and partly because the force of the Government makes us
so to do, so, too, treaties are kept between States, partly because
States recognize it as right to keep their word, partly because if
they break their treaties, the armed force of other communities
will come down upon them. Inside a State, without laws, the
people would be like a pack of wolves ; without treaties independent States would be in the same condition :

> In such condition there is no place for industry, because the
> fruit thereof is uncertain, and consequently no culture of the
> earth ; no navigation, nor use of the commodities that may be
> imported by sea ; no commodious building ; no instruments of
> moving and removing such things as require much force ; no
> knowledge of the face of the earth ; no account of time ; no
> arts ; no letters ; no society ; and which is worst of all, con-
> tinual fear and danger of violent death ; and the life of man,
> solitary, poor, nasty, brutish and short. (Hobbes' *Leviathan*,
> chap. xiii.)

Treaties, and the morality which they enforce, and the International Law which they recognize, save us from this brutish
condition. Treaties are the positive laws of Europe.

§ 2

Inside society individuals' relations have progressed from *status*
to *contract*, that is to say, from the observance of customs to the
observance of positive agreements and laws. States likewise in
their relations with each other have progressed from status to
contract. In the ' Dark Ages ', after the fall of the Roman
Empire, they had no defined international relations other than
those suggested by the accepted morality or immorality of the
time. Usually peoples (they could scarcely be called States) were
not in contact with each other, or if they did touch, they fought.

Thus, wherever the Vikings came, they slew and plundered. Gradually, however, they realized that this condition of affairs could not go on for ever : so they began to make agreements with their enemies, to regulate their ' international relations ' without fighting. So we find in England ' Alfred and Guthrum's Peace ', made in 886, between the West Saxons on the one hand, and, on the other, the Danish invaders who till then had been only a name for cruelty and treachery :

> This is the peace that King Alfred and King Guthrum and the witan of all the English nation, and all the people that are in East Anglia have all ordained and with oaths confirmed, for themselves and for their descendants, as well for born as for unborn, who seek of God's mercy or yours.

Then follow the actual terms : concerning land-boundaries— ' up on the Thames, then up on the Lea, and along the Lea to its source, and thence to Bedford, then up on the Ouse unto Watling Street ' ; and concerning breaches of the peace—' we estimate all equally dear, English and Danish, at eight half-marks of pure gold ' ; and so forth : a truly excellent treaty. A little later the French and Normans made their peace and boundary treaty at Clair-sur-Epte in 911.

After the Normans conquered England, the Anglo-Norman State had territory on both sides of the Channel. This fact gave rise to a long period of warlike relations between France and England, that is, to relations of mere violence, not of law. Gradually, however, a treaty-system grew up between the two countries, although broken, periodically, by long wars. These treaties which provided intervals of law between intervals of violence between France and England were, for example, the Treaty of Paris, 1259, of Bretigny, 1360, of Troyes, 1420. The last-mentioned treaty based Anglo-French relations on the stipulation that the English sovereign was to succeed to the French throne—a stipulation that soon threw the two countries back into the condition of warring atoms. A better system was to come with the close of the Middle Ages.

These Anglo-French treaties, and the other mediaeval treaties, only regulated dealings between pairs of States. They provided no general system of public law. Public law was, to some extent, provided by the accepted customs or rules of chivalry, by the principles of the old Roman Civil Law, and by the Canon Law. The Pope was in a sense the guardian of international morality. But the Reformation and the decay of feudalism destroyed the mediaeval political system, and threw back the States of Europe, not internally, but externally, into a condition of anarchy among themselves. Into this new condition of affairs, this vacuum created by the disruption of the Universal Church, Macchiavelli stepped with principles which for the time being only increased the international anarchy.

§ 3

Macchiavelli had considerable experience of international relations. He had witnessed the invasion of Italy by Charles VIII of France in 1494. Four years later, at the age of twenty-nine, he became secretary of the Florentine Chancery. *Il Principe* was written in the year 1513.

This book has justly been considered to be, after Aristotle's *Politics*, the pioneer work of political science. It treats of Politics as a distinct thing, without any confusion with Ethics or other study. Macchiavelli's theme was *the means for preserving the State*; and with perfect scientific detachment he reviews measures adapted to this end, without considering whether the suggested measures are moral or immoral. Political science benefited from this clear thinking; but it must not be supposed that when Macchiavelli said that certain means were well adapted to ensure the preservation of a State, he therefore thought that they were morally justifiable. It was his business to analyse the preservatives of States ; the moral responsibility lies with those who use them. Thus he says :

> Every one recognizes how praiseworthy it is in a Prince to keep faith, and to act uprightly and not craftily. Nevertheless we see from what has happened in our own days that Princes who have set little store by their word, but have known how to overreach others by their cunning, have accomplished great things, and in the end had the better of those who trusted to honest dealing. (*The Prince*, chap. xviii.)

The point of this passage is that the wicked sometimes, perhaps often, prosper in this world : but there is in it no justification for saying that statesmen ought to do a wicked thing, if by so doing they will preserve their States or increase their power. Nevertheless, Macchiavelli's analysis of the means for the preserving of States was taken to be a recommendation of the use of these means ; and many diplomatists and statesmen have allowed their conduct to be guided according to the ' Macchiavellian ' rules. But this is because man is naturally prone to evil, and it would have happened whether Macchiavelli had written or not.

Throughout the sixteenth century the international anarchy was accentuated by the religious conflicts which arose out of the Reformation. German princes fought against their Emperor. French Huguenots fought against their King, who did not scruple to employ assassination and murder against them. The Dutch, persecuted alike for their political and religious opinions, rose against their Spanish master (1572). Foreign Powers intervened in these domestic struggles, until at last another religious war was started which, being fought more intensely and involving greater political issues than previous religious wars, became a European struggle. This was the Thirty Years War (1618–48) which by its length and bitterness brought the combatants at last to a real conclusion, and has ended religious strife.

It was during this long-drawn-out struggle, when every State was appealing to force and to force alone, that Grotius set himself to think out a new system of public law for Europe. This man arose during the grand years of the foundation and establishing of the Dutch Republic. No nation has made a wiser use of its freedom, no nation has more abundantly justified the claim of nationality. Yet Grotius' own people rejected him; for after having been made historiographer to the Republic in 1603, and after having represented his Government at the English court in the same year, he was imprisoned for his political and religious opinions in 1619, and only escaped in the trunk which ought to have contained the prisoner's books and washing. Henceforth he spent most of his life at Paris, where he was in later years nominated by the Swedish Chancellor, Oxenstierna, as ambassador of Sweden to the French Government. His *De Iure Belli et Pacis* was printed at Paris in 1625, and was sold at the Frankfort Fair, the author just clearing his expenses.

This eminent man, equally distinguished in his own time as a diplomatist, historian, theologian, classical scholar, and lawyer, belongs to the band of fruitful workers who have signally lightened the burden of humanity. If International Law has never been completely observed, neither have the Ten Commandments; it has always stood as an ideal and progressively improving standard of international conduct, and has checked, if it has not been able wholly to control, the evil passions which spread misery among the nations.

Grotius built his system upon the ancient Law of Nations, the *Ius Gentium*. According to Sir Henry Maine,

> The *Ius Gentium* was a collection of rules and principles, determined by observation to be common to the institutions which prevailed among the various Italian tribes. (Maine, *Ancient Law*, chap. iii.)

This celebrated definition has been criticized. Sir Frederick

Pollock has pointed out that ancient codes were not quite so deliberately and scientifically created : they were slow, customary growths, which were only written down and edited long after they had been, partially at any rate, in use. Regarded in this light the Roman *Ius Gentium* was a system of customary law used to regulate dealings among foreigners, or between Romans and foreigners, within the Roman jurisdiction. It was like one of those customary and accepted systems of ' Law Merchant ' which existed during the Middle Ages for instance, in the Mediterranean ports, the Bay of Biscay, or the Baltic. However it was made, this at least is certain, that in old Roman times there was a *Ius Gentium*, and that its rules and principles were applicable and intelligible to men of different race and different cultures. About A.D. 360 the *Ius Gentium* was definitely codified as the Edictum Perpetuum of the Praetor Peregrinus. This codification, however, did not prevent further development and additions at the hands of eminent lawyers and magistrates.

Alongside of the *Ius Gentium*, which was a body of definite legal rules, there was coming into general acceptance in the ancient Roman world a Law of Nature, a *Ius Naturale*. This was supposed to be the common basis of all law.

> The tendency to look not to the past but to the future for types of perfection was brought into the world by Christianity. (*Ancient Law*, chap. iv.)

The Greek philosophers looked not to future ages, nor to the world to come, for their Golden Age ; they put it in the days of long ago : then men were perfect, then was the state of Nature. So, to live according to Nature was the true object of man's life. Out of this view grew the idea that there was a Law of Nature— the reasonable, the just, the equitable—according to which all human intercourse should be regulated. This idea of a Law of Nature, carried from Greece to Rome by the Stoic philosophers, was allowed to modify the Praetorian Edict. Thus the Law of

Nature and the Law of Nations as they existed side by side and to some extent in amalgamation, in the later Roman Empire, came down in various ancient text-books and commentaries, through the Middle Ages, to modern times.

The Law of Nature and the Law of Nations were used together by Grotius : *Ius Naturae* (or *Ius Naturale*), as he understood it from the sayings of ' philosophers, historians, poets, and finally orators ', supplied him with abstract principles : *Ius Gentium* supplied him with certain specific rules which suited the dealings of men of different nations. Thus,

> The greatest function of the Law of Nature was discharged in giving birth to modern International Law. (*Ancient Law*, chap. iv.)

The scaffolding of the Grotian fabric of International Law consists of three postulates. First, that there is a determinable Law of Nature.

> Natural Law is the Dictate of Right Reason, indicating that any act, from its agreement or disagreement with the rational nature of man has in it a moral turpitude or a moral necessity ; and consequently that such an act is forbidden or commended by God, the author of Nature. (*De Iure Belli et Pacis*, trans. Whewell, Bk. I, chap. i, § x.)

The second postulate of the Grotian system is that Natural Law is binding on States in their relations with each other.

> Be it so then that in the conflict of arms, laws must be silent ; but let this be understood of laws civil, judicial, proper to peace ; not of those laws which are perpetual and accommodated to all time. For it is excellently said by Dio Prusaeensis, that between enemies, written laws, that is, Civil Laws, are not in force ; but that unwritten laws are, namely, those which nature dictates, or the consent of nations institutes. (*Ibid.*, Prolegomena, par. 26.)

And if the Law of Nature is binding upon States *inter se*, the States must be regarded as individuals, each of equivalent weight

with the other. ' In International Law the atoms which compose
it must be absolutely equal.' (*Ancient Law*, chap. iv.) This
follows from the second postulate.

The third postulate is that sovereignty is territorial—that is to
say, that sovereigns are in relation to each other like landed pro-
prietors, so that the ordinary morality which forbids cheating,
stealing, assaulting, and such things, holds good between them.

> Let us come to those things which may become property. . . .
> Here two remarks are to be made : first that there are two
> kinds of occupation, in totality, and in particular shares. The
> former is commonly made by the people, or the ruler of the
> people ; the other by individuals. (*De Iure Belli et Pacis*,
> Bk. II, chap. ii.)

Thus Grotius began that body of laws which, through custom, precedents, and agreements, has since grown into so large
a structure. And if this International Law has not yet superseded
war between nations, as municipal law has superseded the duel
among citizens, we must not despair. Grotius has accomplished
much.

> I, holding it to be most certain that there is among nations
> a common law of Rights, which is of force with regard to
> war, and in war, saw many and grave causes why I should write
> a work on that subject. For I saw prevailing throughout the
> Christian world a licence in making war of which even barbarous
> nations would have been ashamed ; recourse being had to
> arms for slight or no reason ; and when arms were once taken
> up, all reverence for divine and human law was thrown away,
> just as if men were thenceforth authorized to commit all crimes
> without restraint. (Prolegomena, par. 28.)

In spite of what people may say, international affairs *have*
improved since Grotius thus described them.

II

The System Founded and Challenged

§ 1

THE Thirty Years War was the last of the religious wars to which the Reformation had given rise in Europe. It began in 1618 with the attempt of the Protestant nobles of Bohemia to substitute the Calvinist Elector of the Palatinate for their Catholic Habsburg king. The war spread throughout Germany, and became a contest between the Reformation and the Counter-Reformation. Foreign Powers intervened: Spain from the beginning took part because she was a great Catholic Power, allied by family ties to Austria; the Dutch joined in the struggle, because they were fighting their War of Independence against Spain; Gustavus of Sweden came in, in 1630, in order to aid his fellow Protestants, and also to keep the Habsburg Empire from extending itself to the Baltic; and in 1634 France, guided by the great Cardinal Richelieu, joined the Swedish side in the war, not indeed with the object of helping Protestantism, but in order to check the power of the Empire and to establish the Rhine frontier. England, owing to the domestic troubles of the first two Stuart kings, took only a very minor part. The war dragged along its wearisome existence until 1648 when, after four years of negotiations (which had not interrupted the hostilities), it was ended by the Peace of Westphalia.

This is the first of the grand settlements of modern European history. Of these there have been four—Westphalia, 1648, ending the Thirty Years War; Utrecht, 1713, ending the Spanish Succession War; Vienna, 1815, ending the Napoleonic War; and Versailles, 1919, ending the 'Great War'. The Peace of Westphalia may be said to have reconstructed the European system which had been in dissolution since the beginning of the Reformation. The three subsequent settlements reconstructed the system after an outbreak of general European war which had temporarily destroyed it.

The Peace of Westphalia consisted of three treaties: one between Spain and the Dutch, dated at Münster, on the 30th January 1648; a second between the Emperor, the King of

France, and Princes of the Empire, at Münster, on the 24th October of the same year; and thirdly a treaty between the Empire and Sweden, also dated the 24th October, but signed at Osnabrück. These three treaties established, among other matters, three things which henceforth may be considered as fundamental, as vital parts of the structure of the European States System. The first thing was a clear adjustment of relations between Catholics and Protestants and the establishing of a *modus vivendi*

between them which has endured till this day, and has prevented any further religious wars. This *modus vivendi* was recognized by Article V of the Osnabrück treaty :

> That there be an exact and reciprocal equality amongst all the Electors, Princes and States of both Religions, conformably to the State of the Commonweal, the Constitution of the Empire, and the present Convention : so that what is just of one side shall be so of the other, all violence and force between the two Parties being for ever prohibited.

Mutual toleration of Catholic and Protestant thus became the law of the Empire ; and although the treaty only referred to the Empire, that is, to the States of Germany, the principle which it contained became a pattern for all northern and, ultimately, for western Europe.

The second thing, which is fundamental to the European System and which was established at Westphalia, was the independence of the Dutch (the United Netherlands or Holland), in the Münster Treaty of the 30th January. Belgium—known then as the Spanish Netherlands—was not independent but remained under the Crown of Spain. Consequential to the establishing of Dutch independence was the fixing of the frontier between the United Netherlands and the Spanish (Belgian) Netherlands.

> Each shall remain effectively in the possession and enjoyment of the countries, towns, forts, lands and dominions which he holds and possesses at present (Art. 3.)

Thus the Belgo-Dutch frontier was established, such as it has, with small modifications, existed to the present day, with the Dutch holding the south side of the estuary of the Scheldt as well as the north side. In addition to this permanent fact in Belgo-Dutch relations, another provision—only temporary, although it lasted for 167 years—was introduced by Article 14.

> The river of the Scheldt, as also the canals of Sas, Zwyn, and other mouths of rivers disemboguing themselves there, shall be kept shut on the side of the Lords of the States.

This is the famous ' Closure of the Scheldt ' which prevented any sea-borne trade from coming to Antwerp throughout the rest of the seventeenth and the eighteenth centuries.

The third fundamental part of this European settlement was the acquisition in full sovereignty by France of a large part of Alsace, and also of Lorraine as a ' sphere of influence ' (it was actually annexed in 1739). The Alsace-Lorraine terms are contained in Articles 72–6 of the Münster treaty of the 24th October. Acts more particularly relating to Lorraine are the Treaty of the Pyrenees, 1559 (Arts. 68–9), and the Treaty of Bar, 1661. It cannot seriously be questioned, now, that it is essential to any stable European system that France should have a firm eastern frontier.

The Treaty of the Pyrenees must be included, as being a kind of pendant to the Peace of Westphalia. Two of the Powers which had engaged in the Thirty Years War did not conclude peace with each other in 1648. These were France and Spain (with Spain's ally, the Duchy of Lorraine). Their war went on till 1659, when Cardinal Mazarin and Don Louis Mendez de Haro signed articles of peace on the Isle of Pheasants in the Bidassoa river, on the confines of the Pyrenees, on the 7th November 1659. Article 42 defined the frontier between the two countries as the Pyrenees :

> The Pyrenean Mountains, which anciently hath divided the Gauls from Spain, shall also make henceforth the division of both the said kingdoms.

The territories ' that be in the said Pyrenean Mountains towards Spain ' were to be in Spanish jurisdiction, while the mountains towards France were to be French. In practice this method of division meant the adoption of the watershed : rivers flowing into Spain water Spanish territory, rivers flowing towards France water the French territory. The Treaty of the Pyrenees has provided the most stable frontier in the European System.

§ 2

The Peace of Westphalia established the modern European States System. It recognized a division of religious power which has, on the whole, been found to be satisfactory. According to this division North Germany and Holland retained their freedom to worship as Protestants ; and with these countries Great Britain and the Scandinavian Powers may be considered as being included, having been involved in the struggle, and being vitally interested in the result. The rest of Europe, except Russia, the Balkans, and Switzerland, was Catholic. Thus by the Peace of Westphalia both the Reformation and the Counter Reformation ceased to be militant. It is true that there were subsequent outbursts of persecution, in France under Louis XIV, and in Salzburg in 1731 ; yet on the whole, in Europe, the two religions agreed to live and let live. Since then there has been no religious war, and there never will be any (between Catholics and Protestants at any rate) unless the balance of religious power, as established at Westphalia, be seriously disturbed.

§ 3

The States System of Europe depends upon an equipoise, a balance of power, so adjusted that each State can keep what it already possesses, and that no one State or group of States shall be able to coerce and despoil the rest. In the absence of any super-State, of any international League or Society of Nations, this balance of power has necessarily been attended to and maintained by the States which themselves make up the States System. Normally each State can look after its own interests, and preserve its independence and its territory. Even a State that has little or no material resources can in normal times rest securely upon the accepted principles of International Law, and be certain that no other State will without provocation assail its independence or rob it of its territories.

Thus for years at a time the European System goes on existing happily enough. Each State keeps what it has, lives at peace with its neighbours, and consumes or exchanges the fruits of its labour. But this halcyon period is unstable : it is always liable to be broken into by some State that takes upon itself to assault the system. This assault comes about, either because a whole people waxes fat and arrogant, or because one or more persons within it become ambitious of conquest, and form designs to extend their State by force. Indeed this ambition to make conquests is not necessarily limited to one State at a time ; it may exist in the breasts of men of several States. Yet, as far as can be discerned, till the present day only one man, set of persons or State has had in any one period both the will and the power to make an assault on the European System.

History shows that since the Peace of Westphalia the States of Europe have enjoyed periods of equilibrium and therefore periods of peace (or of relative peacefulness), which, however, have been every now and then threatened and sometimes destroyed by a Disturber. The appearance of such a Disturber (or of a Disturbing State) has, in turn, always provoked the other States of Europe (or some of them) to band together to defend the system and to check the aggressor. The end of each struggle has usually been that the aggressor has been overcome, and that the European system has been re-established by some general peace-settlement, some treaty on the grand scale, continuing, with the modifications which the struggle has made necessary, the settlement of Westphalia.

Looked at in this light, Louis XIV was a Disturber of the European System, sending his armies like battering rams against the structure reared at the Peace of Westphalia and the Pyrenees. The assaults of Louis XIV provoked coalitions of the assaulted States and of others who showed an interest in the System. After a long series of wars he was finally defeated ; and the European

System was re-established at the Peace of Utrecht in 1713. Passing over smaller wars, we find that the next Disturbers on a grand scale were the French Revolutionary State and its most concrete expression, Napoleon I. These Disturbers, too, provoked a European coalition, which after unparalleled efforts quelled them, and re-established the European System at the Congress of Vienna in 1815. Bismarck, too, through his attack upon Denmark, his destruction of the Germanic Confederation, and the annexation of Alsace and Lorraine, must be counted as a fatal Disturber. Lastly we come to the assault made on the System so dramatically by Germany, when she suddenly invaded France through Belgium in 1914, thus again bringing into action a warlike Coalition of Europe, which, after efforts intenser still than in any previous disturbance, reconstructed the system by the Treaty of Versailles in 1919.

Experience seems to show that no one State can overcome the public opinion and the resources of the rest of Europe. Yet this experience has not deterred disturbers in the past. Therefore it was wise of the Concert Powers, in the last settlement, to reinforce the old system with an additional member, the League of Nations, which perhaps will prevent a new Disturber from taking action in the future.

III

Louis XIV

§ 1

THE European System went through some painful experiences in the Age of Louis XIV. France was a great country and was entitled to make herself secure in Europe ; but the designs of the *Grand Monarque* aimed at much more than mere security. In previous years—in the Middle Ages—the frontiers of France had been deplorably weak. After the opening of the modern era, the French kings had only made the external condition of their State worse by pursuing the will-o'-the-wisp of conquest in Italy. But a change in French foreign policy had come with Henry II (1547–59), who had the strength of mind to give up the Italian dream, and the sagacity to see that France's real interest lay in strengthening her eastern frontier. It was he who gained from the Emperor Charles V the *Trois Évêchés*, the Bishoprics of Metz, Toul, and Verdun, an acquisition which was confirmed and extended at the Peace of Westphalia. The Westphalian annexations of France were the result of the efforts of Cardinals Richelieu and Mazarin; these statesmen adopted and amplified Henry II's ' eastern ' policy, which thus became established as the *système classique*, the tradition of the French foreign office. Writing of the politicians of a later age, of the men of the French Revolution, Sorel thus describes the *système classique* :

Formed by the study of the classics, renewed by the historians, spread broadcast by the men of letters, preserved in the archives of the parliaments, the tradition was thus transmitted to the two classes of men who exercised a dominant influence on the exterior policy of the French Revolution, the lawyers and the soldiers. It came to them singularly clarified and disengaged by the spirit of analysis which was in the air at the time. . . . For the soldiers, the necessities of attack and defence ; for the politician, the necessities of domestic government ; for the diplomatists, the necessities of European peace—these were the only elements in the discussion. All were agreed in defining the extreme limits : Savoy and Nice on one side, the Meuse and Rhine on the other. The acquisition of the left bank of the Rhine was not for any one the direct and definite object of a political design ; it was the ideal object, the proposition of the future, the last term of the series. If people kept this last term in view, it was because it is necessary to have a last term in everything, and because this one seemed to be marked out by geography, by history, by politics. The most simple reflection proved that if it was perhaps dangerous to advance as far as this point, in going beyond it France would certainly exceed the measure of power which is compatible with the balance of forces in Europe ; she would be passing beyond the boundaries of the domain which she can govern, defend, keep. (Sorel, *L'Europe et la Révolution française*, i, pp. 321–2.)

Henry II, Richelieu, and Mazarin had a clear idea of what was moderate and possible : they aimed at the Rhine and the Meuse, the Alps and the Pyrenees. But Louis XIV aimed at going further—to Madrid, Brussels, Amsterdam. He misunderstood the classical system : he exaggerated it till it became a wholly different thing :

> There was in exterior enterprises a certain *measure* beyond which it was necessary not to pass—an excess, which Europe would not have tolerated, and which the French themselves would not have been capable of sustaining. This is the basis of the classical system. *Louis XIV denatured it.* (Sorel, *ibid.*, i. 283.)

Louis XIV's policy of *excess*, which gradually brought against him a coalition of western Europe, began soon after he had reached his majority, which happened in the year 1660. Taking advantage of a naval war which was going on between England and the Dutch, and which therefore seemed to immobilize the two chief Powers who might have checked his enterprise, he suddenly invaded the Spanish Netherlands in 1667, claiming that they devolved upon him in right of his wife, a daughter of the late King of Spain, Philip IV. Soon he would have reached Brussels, and perhaps even the mouths of the Rhine, had not England and the Dutch made peace, and then, in conjunction with Sweden, formed the *Triple Alliance* of the 23rd January 1668. This act, the work of three wise statesmen, Sir William Temple, John de Witt, and Count Christopher Dohna, convinced Louis that he could not assault the European balance against the opposition of the *Maritime Powers.* So he made peace, and abandoned his claim to the Spanish Netherlands, gaining, however, a few highly useful small towns on the north-eastern frontier. (Treaty of Aix-la-Chapelle, 2 May 1668.)

The next assault on the balance came in 1672. Louis had not forgiven the Dutch for having checked his designs on the Spanish Netherlands in 1667. This time he appears to have intended the complete subjugation of the Dutch—an aim which, if successful, would have destroyed the European balance and made France dominant everywhere. For possession of the Low Countries would have given to France control of the Scheldt and of the mouths of the Rhine, the means of easily invading Germany and also England, and possibly the command of the English Channel and the North Sea. The French king's plans were well laid, for he had secured England's alliance by the infamous Secret Treaty of Dover in 1670 (an alliance due to the personal intervention of Charles II) ; and in 1672, before he began the war, he induced the Swedes to make, like the English king, a mercenary alliance. The war started in May, and by the end of summer practically only Amsterdam was left in the hands of the Dutch, and that was only preserved from the enemy by flooding. Then Europe came to the rescue : the Empire, Spain, and the Duchy of Lorraine made military alliances with the Dutch (1673) ; and Charles II was forced by the public opinion of England to withdraw from war against Holland (1674). Four more years of war showed to Louis that he was still not strong enough to defy Europe. So a Peace Conference met at Nymwegen (1678). The Treaties of Nymwegen preserved the balance of power as it had existed before, although Spain had to cede her outlying province of Franche-Comté to France—a gain which cannot be considered as marking that ' excess ' which Europe could not tolerate. The acquisition of Franche-Comté only brought France to one of her natural frontiers, the Jura Mountains. The acquisitions on the frontier of the Spanish Netherlands—Valenciennes, Cambrai, Ypres—were more questionable, as they gave to France a means of continually invading this sensitive spot of Europe. Besides, even if not very dangerous to Europe, France's gains between 1672 and 1678 were the result of pure aggression : ' Europe had never before witnessed such encroachments on the sanctity of the rights of property.' (Heeren, *op. cit.*, p. 142.)

The next war was provoked by extensions of French territorial authority made by Louis XIV under interpretations—French, not international, interpretations—of the Treaties of Nymwegen. By these means he took possession of Strasbourg on the 30th September 1681, as well as of other places. Moreover, he continued in occupation of Lorraine, as the Duke of that country refused to subscribe to the Treaties of Nymwegen. All this provoked the States of Europe to another warlike attempt to resist the French disturber—an effort known as the War of the League of Augsburg (29 July 1686), a League which included the Dutch, Spain, the Emperor, Sweden, Brandenburg, and other German principalities. The patient contriver of this League was William III of Orange, who after the Revolution of 1688 was able to bring England into the struggle, and to bind western Europe in a Grand Alliance (9 December 1689) against France. Yet it required nearly seven more years of war before Louis could be compelled to loose his grip on the Spanish Netherlands ; and when peace was at last made at the Congress of Ryswick on the 20th September 1697 France had to be allowed to retain Strasbourg.

The result of these wars was that the King of France had failed to overthrow the balance of power ; but in his efforts to do so, while failing in the wider aim, he had gained a lesser object—he had greatly strengthened the frontier of France. He had pushed the north-eastern boundary forward by the acquisition of Lille, Valenciennes, Armentières, Cambrai, and other places ; and by getting Strasbourg and thus completing the acquisition of Alsace, as well as by occupying Lorraine, he had brought his country to the left bank of the Rhine. Very soon Alsace and Lorraine were reconciled to the French sovereignty, and became an integral part of France. But the German national historians of the nineteenth century came to look upon Alsace-Lorraine as a sort of *terra irredenta*, to be won back at the point of the sword. That is why Ranke meeting Thiers in Vienna during the war of 1870 said : ' it is not France that we are fighting against, but Louis XIV.'

§ 2

The French wars of 1667–97 show Europe gradually becoming conscious that it was a System of States, in which no one member could think of itself as an isolated unit. Yet this consciousness was by no means complete. Its chief promoter was William III. The statesmanship of this great man was on European lines : his view was not bounded by any narrow conception of the interest of Britain or Holland, but by a survey of at least all western Europe ; he had the breadth of mind to see that the good of Britain and Holland was the good of the whole European System.

It was to preserve this system that he now laboured in the few years of life that were left to him after the conclusion of the Peace of Ryswick. For Charles II of Spain was dying childless, and his vast empire was likely to be claimed in entirety by Louis XIV on the one hand, and by Leopold I of Austria on the other, for each of these sovereigns had married sisters of the Spanish king. The European States System would be practically at the mercy of any Power, whether Austria or France, that obtained the Spanish Empire ; and such a contingency would inevitably provoke a great war, a gigantic, costly, and perhaps fruitless effort, on the part of the remaining States, to preserve the balance of power. The only way to prevent such a European war was to arrange beforehand with the claimants to the Spanish Empire that they should agree to some equitable scheme for peacefully disposing of it. It was with this aim in view that William III thought out an elaborate scheme for partitioning the Spanish Empire, and that he laboured to obtain the consent of all claimants. The Partition Treaties of 1698 and 1700 were not arbitrary acts of egotistic politicians 'cutting up States as merchants cut Dutch cheeses'; they were beneficent projects designed to do justice all round, to avoid effusion of blood, and to preserve the European System. The basis of each Partition Treaty was that the kingdom of Spain itself should be kept entire; so, to this extent at any rate, the national pride of the Spanish people was not disregarded.

The First Partition Treaty (1698), an eminently statesmanlike instrument, was to the effect that Spain, the Indies, and the Netherlands should on the death of Charles II pass to the Electoral Prince of Bavaria; France was to be satisfied with Naples, Sicily, and Guipuscoa; Austria was to get Milan. The Treaty became void because the Electoral Prince died young. The Second Partition Treaty (1700) was much more difficult to conclude: its object was simply to divide the Spanish Dominions between France and the House of Austria: France to get Milan, Naples, Sicily, and Guipuscoa, while the second son of Leopold I of Austria was to get Spain itself, the Indies, and the Netherlands. Milan was subsequently to be transferred to the Duke of Lorraine by France, in exchange for Lorraine itself. Louis XIV agreed to all this; but Austria did not. It was really the refusal of Austria that brought the subsequent troubles upon Western Europe.

In November 1700 Charles II of Spain died leaving a will, which his Councillors knew and approved of. This will stipulated that the Spanish Dominions must not be divided; that they were to be offered to the second grandson of Louis XIV; and that if refused by the House of France, they were to be offered to the other claimant, the House of Austria.

If Louis XIV had kept to the Partition Treaty which he had

signed, and if he had rejected the will of Charles II, then the whole Spanish inheritance would have passed to the House of Austria, which had not signed the Partition Treaty and therefore was not bound by it. Indeed Louis may reasonably have held that France's adhesion to the Partition Treaty (which was a sort of

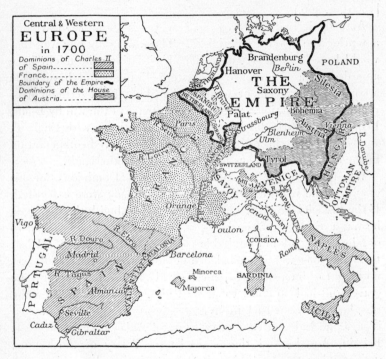

Central & Western
EUROPE
in 1700
Dominions of Charles II of Spain
France
Boundary of the Empire
Dominions of the House of Austria

self-denying ordinance) was conditional upon the other interested party, Austria, observing it. Therefore, as Austria would not join in the Partition, and would probably have accepted the whole Spanish inheritance, if the offer had been made, Louis XIV, after much searching of heart in council with his Ministers, agreed to accept the Spanish Dominions for his second grandson. The will of Charles II stipulated that France and Spain should never be joined together : but Louis XIV evidently thought otherwise, for when his grandson was setting out for his new realm the old king embraced the young man affectionately, with the words : '*Adieu, mon fils ; il n'y a plus de Pyrénées.*' (*Œuvres de Louis XIV* [1806], ii. 466.)

Actually it is difficult to see how Louis could have avoided accepting the Spanish Dominions. There was only one way that would have led him out of a difficult situation : he might have appealed to a Conference of western Europe, and have made a concerted arrangement with all the States for a settlement of the Spanish succession. After the acceptance of the will by Louis, Leopold of Austria did in fact enter into a treaty with England, agreeing to waive his claims to Spain, if he received compensation in the Spanish Dominions in Italy and the Netherlands.

When Louis XIV accepted the Spanish Dominions for his grandson the resources of European diplomacy were exhausted. If the French king really meant politically to abolish the Pyrenees, he was a disturber of the European System. So having failed to obtain a peaceful and equitable partition, King William III had to face a long war for a balance of power which, after all, was nothing to him personally, for he had already one foot in the grave, and had no child to succeed him. Cold and harsh as he was, he never went back in his sense of duty ; and before he died in 1702 he had created a second Grand Alliance between Great Britain, Austria, and the Netherlands (Treaty of the Hague, 7 September 1701). This subsequently included practically all the States of western Europe except the enemy France and her only ally Bavaria.

The War of the Spanish Succession went on for ten years, until two things became apparent : that France, although not winning the war, would not be conquered ; and that Spain would never accept another king than Philip V, the grandson of Louis XIV.

In truth the Allies had not begun the war to prevent this, but to detach so much of its outlying dominions from Spain as would make for a satisfactory balance of power. Article 5 of the Treaty of the Hague, 7 September 1701 (the Grand Alliance), stated the object of the war to be:

> To recover the Provinces of the Spanish Low Countries, that they may be a fence and rampart, commonly called a Barrier, separating and distancing France from the United Provinces . . . ; as likewise the Duchy of Milan, with its dependencies, as a Fief of the Empire, and contributing to the security of his Imperial Majesty's hereditary Countries; besides the kingdom of Naples and Sicily, and the lands and islands upon the Coasts of Tuscany, in the Mediterranean, that belong to the Spanish Dominions, and may serve to the same purpose; and will also be of advantage to the navigation and commerce of the subjects of the King of Great Britain, and of the United Provinces.

The Peace Congress met at Utrecht in the United Netherlands on the 29th January 1712 and concluded its labours in midsummer 1713. On the 11th April 1713 seven treaties were signed by France on the one part and her enemies (except the Emperor, who acceded later) on the other. These treaties put into the public law of Europe the designs which William III had in mind when he formed the Grand Alliance against France. Philip V was recognized as King of Spain, but Article 6 of the Anglo-French treaty states:

> the most destructive flame of war which is to be extinguished by this peace arose chiefly from hence, that the Security and Liberties of Europe could by no means bear the Union of the Kingdoms of France and Spain under one and the same King:

and accordingly it incorporates mutual renunciations by Philip V and by the heirs to the French throne.

In Article IV France acknowledges the rights of succession to England 'of the Protestant line of Hanover'. Many other

important conditions were made with regard to colonial power, as well as to European territory. In Europe a most significant condition was made by the Franco-Dutch Treaty of the Utrecht settlement: the Spanish Netherlands were to be handed over to Austria, in order that that State might hold this nodal point in the balance of power safely for the common good of Europe. Moreover, the retrocession of Ypres and Tournai by Louis XIV (to the Austrian Netherlands) weakened the north-eastern frontier of France, but on the other hand she was permitted to keep her former conquest, Lille (Art. 16). Two subsequent treaties completed the Utrecht settlement. An Anglo-Spanish Treaty, dated Utrecht, 13 July 1713, contains the cession of Gibraltar to Great Britain, with the right of pre-emption to Spain if Great Britain ever wishes to sell or alienate it. Lastly, by the Franco-Austrian Treaty of Rastadt (6 March 1714) the Emperor agreed to accept the Spanish Netherlands and also Naples, Sardinia, and Milan.

Thus the balance of power was re-established. Bourbon princes reigned at Paris and Madrid, but the two crowns must never be joined together. Italy was put under the guardianship of Austria, as was also the 'Belgian' (i. e. the former Spanish, now to be called the Austrian) Netherlands. To make security greater in these Netherlands the Dutch were to garrison the Austrian fortresses on the French border—Namur, Tournai, Menin, Ypres, Furnes, Warneton, and Knoque. The closure of the Scheldt below Antwerp, as established in the Treaty of Münster, was re-affirmed (Anglo-Dutch-Austrian Treaty of Utrecht, Antwerp, 15 November 1715). Article 17 contained a formal guarantee by Great Britain of all these provisions which related to the Austrian Netherlands.

NOTE.—The idea that the Peace of Westphalia settled finally the religious balance of power in Europe is not new. See Laforest (ambassador in Berlin) to Talleyrand, 17 Dec. 1802: 'The Peace of Westphalia has terminated the religious quarrels, and fixed a *status quo*, Catholic and Protestant (*Archives des Affaires étrangères* Correspondance politique, Allemagne, 720).

IV

The System Tested

§ 1

THE Peace of Utrecht is the second stage in the structure of
the European System. As Treitschke, one of the most suggestive
of historians and publicists, writes :

> Although the mediaeval Christian world possessed the vision
> of an ideal unity, the interests of the different States were in
> actual fact severed by difficulties of communication and back-
> wardness of civilization. A community of interests, or a System
> of States, were still undeveloped. A war might go on for
> a hundred years between Germans and Italians, quite distinct
> from a contemporaneous struggle between English and French,
> without the remaining Powers having any idea of intervening.
> The idea of a practical comity of States had not yet penetrated
> into the flesh and blood of the nations. (*Politik*, trans. Dugdale
> and de Bille, ii. 567–8.)

At the end of the Thirty Years War, international comity was,
to a certain extent, established :

> In the seventeenth century the Congress of the Peace of
> Westphalia offered the astonishing spectacle of a Conference of
> Ambassadors from every State, laying down the frontiers for the
> individual countries. This Peace of Westphalia came to be
> looked upon like a *ratio scripta* of International Law : every one
> uttered thanksgiving that some sort of *status quo* had now been
> established. People began to feel themselves part of an organ-
> ized European society, and all the sovereign States began, as
> it were, to form one great family. (*Ibid.*, 570.)

The Peace of Westphalia certainly represents a tendency
towards international comity, towards the recognition of a
European States System : but the recognition was very far from
complete. The period from 1648 to 1715 shows not merely

a great Disturber trying to break down the System; it also witnessed two European wars on the grand scale going on side by side, and yet not being merged into one and the same struggle. While the Grand Alliance was fighting desperately against Louis XIV in the west, in the north and east Charles XII of Sweden was contending for over twenty years against Peter the Great of Russia and the Saxons, Danes, and Poles.

> The great drama of the Scandinavian War was being played out at the same time in the eastern half of Europe, but the two contests had no connexion with each other, and are therefore not to be described as European (*Ibid.*, p. 573).

After 1714 this dualism in Europe was impossible. The Treaties of Utrecht extended and adapted the Westphalia settlement to the growth of the European States. Utrecht was always regarded as a *European* settlement, and it remained as the core of the States System for the next two hundred years. After 1714, if wars were to arise, there could, at any rate, only be one war on the grand scale at the same time. In the struggles that took place immediately after the Utrecht settlement—the war of Austria against Turkey (1715–18), of Sweden against Russia (1715–21), and of Spain against France and England (1717–18), the diplomatists of all Europe were busy, and in the final settlements the good offices of third parties were admitted. If these three struggles did not actually form one war, they were at least connected with each other. And the next war on the grand scale which occurred—the War of the Polish Succession (1733–9)—did involve almost all the Powers, both those who were directly interested in Poland and those who were not. Only one great Power did not take part, England, then administered by the sagacious Walpole. England's abstention from the struggle was owing to the French Government's having given Walpole a guarantee by Treaty that the neutrality of the Austrian Netherlands would be observed. For the moment, therefore, England was still able to regard herself as an island, and Walpole was able to say to Queen Caroline, ' Madame, fifty thousand men killed this year in Europe, and not one of them an Englishman ! ' It was the last time that such a boast could be made.

§ 2

Until the accession of Frederick II to the throne of Prussia, the System of Europe was not greatly disturbed, in spite of four wars, the most serious being the Polish Succession War. In 1739 a colonial-commercial dispute of long standing between England and Spain came to a head, and produced the maritime ' War of Jenkins's Ear ', fought entirely in South American waters. The English premier, Walpole, was extremely loth to enter upon this contest, because he knew that it could not be localized : English frigates might bombard Spanish-American ports, and chase silver cargoes in the Caribbean Sea ; but the little war would come like a breeze across the sea to Europe and rekindle the embers of continental strife.

Perhaps the war in the Caribbean Sea could have been limited to that area (as a brief war between England and Spain in the year 1727 was localized) had not Frederick II of Prussia chosen at this moment to invade the Austrian province of Silesia. But a mischance of this kind must be held to be almost normal in any time of crisis : it is a characteristic of the modern States System that when any two European States start fighting, some other party, interested or uninterested, is almost sure to join the struggle. Walpole could not know in 1739 that Frederick of Prussia would invade Silesia. But he did know that the reigning Bourbon houses of France and Spain had in 1733 made a Family Compact assuring each other of mutual assistance in their time of need, and that therefore the Anglo-Spanish War would probably become an Anglo-French war too. He knew also that Charles VI of Austria might die at any moment, and that there might be trouble with regard to the succession of Charles's heir, a daughter, Maria Theresa. It is true that an Austrian law of 1713 (the *Pragmatic Sanction*) had altered the law of succession established by the previous emperor, in order to make Maria Theresa the heiress of the whole of the Austrian dominions. Great Britain had guaranteed this, by treaty (Vienna, 16 March 1731). Prussia was also a guarantor (Treaty of Berlin, 23 December 1728) : so were Spain and France. Yet who could be sure that all the Powers would honour their pledge ? On the 20th October 1740 the Emperor Charles VI died. Maria Theresa succeeded peacefully to all the Habsburg territories, and for a month all was well ; but in December Frederick II of Prussia sent his army over the frontier into Silesia.

> The evils produced by his wickedness were felt in lands where the name of Prussia was unknown ; and in order that he might rob a neighbour whom he had promised to defend, black men fought on the coast of Coromandel, and red men scalped each other by the Great Lakes of North America. (Macaulay, *Frederick the Great*.)

The invasion of Silesia by Prussia precipitated a struggle for the dismemberment of Austria. On the 18th May 1741 France, Bavaria, and Spain (Saxony joining later) made a confederacy ; and from almost every point of the compass Austrian dominions were subjected to attack. Only Great Britain, under the compulsion of King George II, remained true to her guarantee of the Pragmatic Sanction, and entered the war on the side of Austria. The result of the long struggle that now ensued was that Maria Theresa had to acquiesce in the cession of most of Silesia to Prussia, and in the loss of some of her Italian territory : but as a whole the Austrian Empire was left as a powerful and integral part of the European System. The Congress which concluded the War of the Austrian Succession met at Aix-la-Chapelle in 1748. The Treaty of Aix-la-Chapelle between all the belligerent Powers (except Frederick of Prussia, who went out of the war with his plunder in 1745) was made on the 30th April, and included the recognition and guarantee of Silesia to Prussia.

Thus an end was put, by this peace, to the project of over-throwing the existing System of Europe, by the dismemberment of Austria. It lost Silesia, Parma and Piacenza, but it kept its station as one of the Great Powers : and it gained, in a short time, a rich compensation for its losses, by a better use of its vast internal resources. (Heeren, *op. cit.*, p. 235.)

The European System had been maintained, but the invasion and seizure of Silesia, though condoned, by force of circumstances, at the Congress of Aix-la-Chapelle, had given it a great shock. In its effect upon the public law of Europe the invasion of Silesia in 1740 has something in common with the invasion of Belgium in 1914.

§ 3

After the Silesian Wars (which were the Prussian aspect of the War of the Austrian Succession) Frederick II set himself to repair his losses and to reorganize his dominions. In 1752, with the help of his able French secretary Darget, he wrote (in French) his Political Testament, a treatise, for the guidance of his successors, on internal administration and on external affairs. The work has three chief parts—one on finance and economy, one on military matters, and a third on policy : this last is an admirable exposition of the views of enlightened Junkerdom.

Politics is the science of acting always by convenient means conformably to one's own interest. To act conformably to one's interests, it is necessary to know what they are ; and to arrive at this knowledge requires study, research and application. The politics of sovereigns have two parts : one, which is concerned with internal government, comprises the interests of the State and the maintenance of its system of government ; the other, which embraces all the System of Europe, labours to consolidate the safety of the State and to extend as much as is possible by customary and permitted means the number of its possessions, the power and the consideration of the prince. (*Die politischen Testamente der Hohenzollern*, Band II, p. 33.)

Here Frederick properly recognizes that there is a European System, but he defines the policy of the State, in a way which is quite incompatible with that System, as an unceasing effort to aggrandize itself—a process which can only be accomplished at the expense of its neighbours, and which therefore is ceaselessly antagonistic to the existing European System of States. It is, moreover, an effort which, unless men become cowards and despair of preserving the System, will never be for long successful : for every effort to subvert the European System calls up a counter-effort to defend it : and no one Power has in the long run been able to defy the rest of Europe.

Yet the Prussians had unsuspected qualities for carrying out their great task of expansion. They are not rigid and narrow : their spirit is subtle, wide, adaptive : *J'ai remarqué que les Prussiens ont l'esprit fin et délié*, says Frederick. He himself was perfectly open-minded : *Je suis neutre entre Rome et Genève*. The States of Europe are all selfish, said Frederick. ' Austria has not forgotten Silesia ' : all the other minor States of Germany are ready to be enemies of Prussia. The interests of Russia are not naturally hostile to those of Prussia, but she may be induced to make an attack.

Russia ought not to count herself among our real enemies : she has no conflict of interest with us ; she is only an accidental enemy. (*Ibid.*, p. 53.)

The two States which really count in Europe are France and England. ' In spite of the abuses of the administration, France is the most powerful State in Europe. Her views of aggrandizement are to extend her limits to the Rhine.' England is potent by reason of her wealth, and by reason of the venality of the German States.

A king of England crosses the sea with a sack of guineas, and moderate sums suffice to corrupt the most powerful Princes of the Germanic Body. (*Ibid.*, p. 54.)

And, adds Frederick, in one of the most emphatic passages in the book :

Christian Europe is like a Republic of Sovereigns which is divided into two great parties. England and France have for a century given the impulse to all movements. When a warlike Prince wishes to undertake anything, if both Powers are in agreement to keep the peace, they will offer their mediation to him, and compel him to accept it. Once it is established, the political System prevents all great robberies and makes war unfruitful unless it be urged with greater resources and extraordinary luck. (*Ibid.*, p. 54.)

The political System to which the great Frederick refers in these last lines is the European equilibrium, the balance of power, supported by concord of France and England. This balance of power is not perfectly rigid : with the passage of time circumstances change, and it is inevitable that modifications should take place in frontiers. But it is in the interests of peace that the grand outlines of the European States should remain the same. Accomplished facts must be accepted. Silesia is to Prussia as Lorraine is to France :

Lorraine and Silesia are like two sisters, of whom one has married the King of Prussia, the other the King of France. (*Ibid.*)

The annexation of Silesia to Prussia was, since the Treaty of Aix-la-Chapelle, a fact in the European System ; but the principle of balance, and of each Power keeping what it had, also remained the essence of the System. We may leave the *Testament politique* with this striking sentence :

The conquest of Silesia is like the books, of which the originals succeed and all the imitations fail. (*Ibid.*, p. 55.)

In the Seven Years War (1756–63), in which all the Powers of Europe took part, Frederick had a desperate fight to keep his Silesia. This time England was on his side, not indeed out of any enmity towards Austria, with whom she never declared war, but because she was involved in a colonial struggle with France. Austria had asked for the alliance of France, in order to gain support in a war for the recovery of Silesia. France accepted, and so the famous Diplomatic Revolution was made. Great Britain, requiring an ally, joined with Prussia. The result of the Seven Years War was that frontiers in Europe remained exactly the same : Prussia retained Silesia ; the balance of power remained as it was after the Congress of Aix-la-Chapelle. But Canada and the control of Bengal had passed from French to English hands. The European States System was throwing forth world-wide ramifications.

§ 4

The wound caused by the seizure of Silesia was cicatrized, but the idea of seizing territories remained. In 1764 Frederick had made an alliance with Russia, as a guarantee against any fresh attack on him by Austria. In 1768 a war occurred between Russia and Turkey, two antagonists who always had causes of strife. Frederick was not called upon to take any part in this, though he paid some subsidies to Russia. The Russian arms were successful, and by the year 1770 only the Danube kept General Rumiantsov out of Bulgaria. But Austria was on the look out against Russian aggrandizement in the Balkan area, and would inevitably declare war if the Russian army crossed the Danube. An Austro-Russian war would bring in Prussia on the Russian side, and France (still allied to the Habsburgs) on the Austrian. The question of Silesia would be re-opened, and there would be a European conflagration, in which Prussia might disappear. Frederick wanted no such conflagration, and he thought of a simple plan. This was to revive an idea, which had been mooted in the

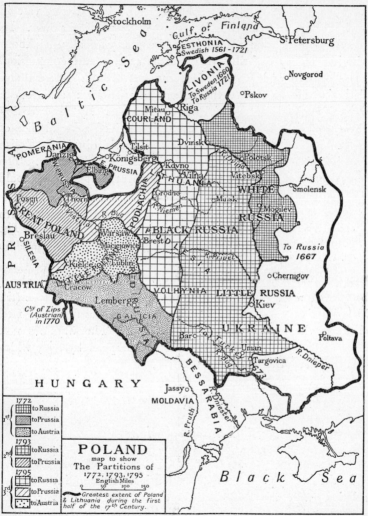

POLAND
map to show
The Partitions of
1772, 1793, 1795
English Miles

Stockholm

Gulf of Finland

St Petersburg

ESTHONIA
Swedish 1561-1721

LIVONIA
To Sweden 1660
To Russia 1721

Novgorod

Baltic Sea

Pskov

Mitau Riga

COURLAND

Dvinsk

Polotsk

POMERANIA
Danzig

Tilsit

Konigsberg

Kovno

R. Dvina

Vitebsk

WHITE

Smolensk

Elbing

E PRUSSIA

Vilna

LITHUANIA

PRUSSIA

Wis

Posen

Thorn

R. Niemen

Grodno

Minsk

RUSSIA

Mogilev

Breslau

GREAT POLAND

R. Bug

BLACK RUSSIA

To Russia
1667

SILESIA

Warsaw

Maciejowice

Brest

SILESIA

R. Pripet

AUSTRIA

Kielce

Lublin

Chernigov

Cracow

Cty of Zips
(Austrian)
in 1770

Lemberg

GALICIA

VOLHYNIA

LITTLE RUSSIA

Kiev

Poltava

Bar

UKRAINE

R. Bug

Uman

Targovica

R. Dnieper

HUNGARY

Jassy

MOLDAVIA

BESSARABIA

R. Pruth

R. Dniester

Black Sea

1772
to Russia
to Prussia
to Austria

1793
to Russia
to Prussia

1795
to Russia
to Prussia
to Austria

50 100 150

Greatest extent of Poland
& Lithuania during the first
half of the 17th Century.

Clarendon Preß, Oxford.

seventeenth century, to partition Poland. This State, vast in territory, was contemptible in respect of its physical power. Its anarchic constitution placed it at the mercy of any neighbour who had money to bribe with, and an army to use compulsion. The Austrian and Russian Governments—Maria Theresa and Catherine II—agreed to the scheme of partition : a European war was avoided, but Poland was the sacrifice. By the Partition Treaty of the 5th August 1772 Russia received a broad slice of eastern Poland, Austria got Galicia. Prussia obtained ' Polish Prussia ', thus connecting Pomerania with Ost-Preussen. The central mass of Poland was left independent, but any one could see that its ultimate fate was sealed.

> But what were the consequences to Poland, in comparison with those which threatened the political system of Europe ? The potentates themselves had begun its subversion. (Heeren, *op. cit.*, p. 315.)

The guardians of the European System did nothing : England, because alone she could not control eastern Europe ; France (the historic friend of Poland), because she was bound in the fatal chain of the Habsburg-Bourbon Alliance. The way was now cleared for the collapse of the whole European System, which occurred after the French Revolution.

V

The Revolution

§ 1

In the twenty years before the French Revolution, international relations were unstable, but there was no general war. The European System gained an extended horizon, for between 1775 and 1783 the United States of America were coming into existence as an independent Power. In the war between Great Britain and the American colonies, France and Spain both took part on the American side ; and the independence of the United States was finally recognized with the Treaty of Versailles, between France, Spain, the United States, and Great Britain, on the 3rd September 1783.

This war marked another important development in international relations, an increasing appreciation of maritime affairs. The neutral States who either carried goods or whose goods were carried at sea resented the restrictions imposed on them by the British fleet in its efforts to prevent trading with the American enemy. So an Armed Neutrality (1780) was formed, a league of Russia, Denmark, Sweden, Prussia, Austria, and Portugal. The chief claim of the Armed Neutrality was the old assertion that the neutral flag covers enemy goods, excepting contraband of war ; and contraband was defined as being arms and munitions of war. The British Government did not commit itself to an admission of this principle ; and the league came to an end when peace was established in 1783.

A grave risk of international conflict occurred in the year after the Peace of Versailles. Austria had possessed the ' Belgian ' Netherlands since the Treaty of Utrecht of 1713, but was bound by the same limitation as had been imposed upon Spain (when Spain held these Netherlands), under the Treaty of Münster (Westphalia), 1648 ; this limitation was the closure of the Scheldt below Antwerp where it passed through Dutch territory. In 1784 the Emperor Joseph II gave orders to an Austrian warship to sail down the Scheldt from Antwerp. Guns from the Dutch fort Saeftingen fired upon the ship and stopped it. Joseph II delivered an ultimatum to the Dutch, and called upon his ally France for support. His design to open the Scheldt to maritime commerce was in itself reasonable but was wholly against Austria's treaty obligations, and to attempt to bring this about by his own action, without asking the consent of the Powers who were responsible for the Westphalia settlement, was really a reckless and perfidious attack on the European States System. Joseph's own Chancellor, Prince Kaunitz, had warned him that a general war would probably ensue from this action; and France, when called upon for military assistance, only offered ' good offices '. Joseph II was checked, and accepted the French mediation. The Treaty of Fontainebleau between Austria and Holland (8 November 1785) reaffirmed the closure of the Scheldt while securing certain advantages to Austria.

Joseph II was a reformer with many good ideas, but he was inclined to be restless. In 1785—the same year as the Scheldt incident was ' closed '—he revived an old plan of his for acquiring Bavaria. This time he wished to give the Austrian Netherlands in exchange. The Elector of Bavaria consented, and if all had gone well he would have been established at Brussels as ' King of Burgundy ', while Austria, uniting with Bavaria, would have become more German and less Slavonic. The plan was quite in conformity with the existing European equilibrium, and possibly neither the inhabitants of Bavaria nor of the Austrian Netherlands would have objected. The House of Wittelsbach, transplanted to the ' Belgian ' Netherlands, would probably have developed into a thoroughly national dynasty there, just as the House of Hanover did in England or, later, the House of Coburg in Belgium. But it was not to be. Frederick the Great crowned a long life of opposition to the House of Habsburg by opposing the ' Bavarian exchange ' plan, so that Joseph II had to drop it (1786). Then Frederick the Great died, leaving on the verge of ruin the European System which he had done so much to enfeeble.

The last flutter in the European System was made by the ancient French monarchy before it went down in the storm of the Revolution.

An old dispute in the United Netherlands between the Party which favoured the House of Orange, and the Party which upheld the rights of the separate States of the Dutch Republic, came to a head in 1786. The Stadtholder, who was the head of the House of Orange, was removed from his office. The ' States ' Party had already entered into alliance with France, which thus gained political ascendancy in the United Netherlands. This was against the interests of Great Britain and of the whole European System, which required that neither the United nor the ' Belgian ' Netherlands, i. e. the mouths of the Scheldt and Rhine, should ever come under the control of a great maritime Power. To prevent this has been the chief aim of all the great wars of modern times—the war of 1702–13 against Louis XIV, the war of 1793–1814 against Revolutionary and Napoleonic France, the war of 1914–18 against Germany. Great Britain, administered by the pacific Pitt, was prepared even to embark on a European war in 1787, but France—wiser under the monarchy than she proved to be four years later under the Republic—declined the contest. A Prussian Corps, with the diplomatic support of England, occupied Holland, and the House of Orange was restored to the Stadtholderate. Next year, a Triple Alliance was made between Great Britain, Prussia, and Holland, guaranteeing the independence of Holland under the hereditary Stadtholder (15 April 1788). Thus the nodal point of the European System seemed to be thoroughly secured.

§ 2

In the summer of 1789 the French Revolution broke forth. On the 21st January 1793 Louis XVI was guillotined. For a year before this, however, he had been powerless and practically a prisoner. The ancient governments of Europe could scarcely be disinterested spectators of his sad condition. Yet the solicitude of the monarchs of Europe for their brother Louis was useless or worse than useless. The threats sent to Paris from the Austrian Chancellery only inflamed the Girondin Government. On the

20th April 1792 they declared war upon Austria. The Prussian Government, feeling equally interested in the fate of Louis XVI, joined in the war on the side of the Habsburgs.

Although the initiative in declaring war came from France, the Austro-Prussian Governments were undoubtedly all along hostile to the Revolution. In this attitude they had some reason on their side, for the French Revolutionary Government had been careless of the vested rights of people who were not French subjects. The abolition of feudal rights, which had been legally accomplished in France by an internal law, could not by any recognized system of law or morality be applied to foreigners, whose rights were secured by treaty. In Alsace many German princes, such as the rulers of Baden, Hesse, Nassau, and the Electors of Mayence, Trèves, and Cologne, had properties, held under ancient feudal law, which were guaranteed to them by the Treaty of Münster (Westphalia), 1648. When France abolished feudal tenures among her own people, it was obviously necessary that she should take steps to bring the proprietary rights of treaty-protected foreigners into conformity with the new law; but those steps should have been taken after previous arrangement with the interested parties. Arbitrarily to deprive the imperial princes of their feudal rights in Alsace was to strike at the foundations of peaceful international relations : in the Revolutionary period France had to learn that peaceful international relations can only subsist when the rights of private property and the sanctity of contracts are mutually recognized.

Thus the first way in which the French Revolutionary Government seriously injured the European System was by repudiating an international contract contained in the Peace Treaties of Westphalia. The second way was by engaging in propaganda against the social and political organization of neighbouring States. France had a right to claim that she would not be dictated to, in choosing her form of government, by foreign States ; but she was equally

bound not to interfere in those States' own form of government. Interference by outside parties in the domestic affairs of States is obviously incompatible with the maintenance of friendly international relations. Yet the orators of the Constituent Assembly in 1790—Pétion, Barnave, Robespierre—were proclaiming 'France's imprescriptible and natural right to reunite the peoples whom her propaganda was freeing' (Bourgeois, *Manuel historique de Politique étrangère*, ii. 37). In September 1792 the same thing was stated more bluntly after France had conquered the Low Countries and annexed Savoy :

> In the name of France, the Constituent Assembly will accord fraternity and succour to all peoples who wish to recover their liberty : it charges the executive power to give to the generals the necessary orders to carry help to those peoples, and to defend their citizens who shall suffer for the cause of liberty. (Decree of 19 November 1792, *ibid.*, p. 83.)

Repudiation of international contract : propaganda to subvert the existing organization in neighbour States : the annexation of Savoy, a regular and useful member of the European States system : the conquest of the Low Countries : and the declaration that the Scheldt was henceforth open to maritime navigation (November 1792)—all these things constituted an attack upon the European System, which the guardians of the System—the great civilized Powers of Europe—were bound to defend.

The opening of the Scheldt to navigation from the sea, was like many other acts of the French Revolutionary Government, in itself reasonable and generally beneficial. But it was carried out in an arbitrary fashion, by sheer force, without reference to the parties who had signed the Treaty of Münster. The European War had, however, begun before the invasion of Belgium by the French.

By the end of 1792 Prussia and Austria were already in the war. The invasion of the Low Countries and the opening of the Scheldt would have brought England in likewise (under the Triple Alliance of 1788), when the French Government anticipated Pitt by themselves declaring war in February 1793.

The First Coalition, of Austria, Prussia, and Great Britain, was not able to prevent the collapse of the existing territorial System of Europe; and this collapse was due not merely to the efforts of France but largely also to faults among some of the Powers who were loudly proclaiming themselves the defenders of the System. Before Great Britain came into the war, the Austrians and Prussians invaded France, but the Prussian army was checked at the ' cannonade of Valmy ' on the 20th September 1792. Of the French artillerymen at Valmy it might be said, as Emerson wrote of the American farmers at Concord, they fired a shot that was heard round the world. The forces of legitimism retired before the forces of Revolution, but the real reason for the Prussian withdrawal was that King Frederick William II wanted to seize another slice of Poland before Russia should absorb all that was left of it. So he and Catherine II took two enormous shares by the Second Partition Treaty of the 4th January 1793. Prussia obtained Posen, Danzig, and Thorn. Austria was left out of the division altogether. There was still something left of Poland; and Austria was naturally resolved that when the inevitable final Partition came about she should not be left again out in the cold. The Third Partition required a regular war, just when the Powers should have been looking after the European System in the west. In 1794 a Russian army invaded Poland: the Poles fought well under General Kosciusko, but in January 1795 their last king had perforce to abdicate. The State was divided again: Austria got Cracow, Prussia Warsaw, the Russians rounded off their western frontier. Nothing at all of Poland was now left : ' Freedom shrieked when Kosciusko fell.' The French Revolutionary armies, even without Bonaparte, profited from these diversions of the Great Powers' strength and interest. After the advent of Bonaparte to high command in 1796 the European System received further blow upon blow. In 1804 Bonaparte made himself Emperor; and two years later the Emperor Francis renounced the crown of the Holy Roman Empire, and henceforth reigned as Emperor of Austria.

§ 3

The astonishing success of the French arms showed that the prospect of European domination by one nation, a prospect against which the Powers have so often fought, was no mere bogey. By the year 1810 all western Europe (except the British Isles), and a great part of central Europe, was directly or indirectly ruled by one man, a military autocrat, Napoleon. The great Napoleonic treaties had disintegrated old Europe in its western and central areas. The Treaty of Campo Formio (17 October 1797, between France and Austria) had destroyed the political system of Italy by annexing the Republic of Venice to Austria, and by recognizing the creation of the Cisalpine and Ligurian Republics (French Protectorates) out of the Milanese, Genoa, and certain other territories. The treaty also ceded the Austrian Netherlands to France, and gave her as an eastern boundary nearly all the left bank of the Rhine from Bâle downwards. The Treaty of Lunéville (9 February 1801, between France and Austria) completed the provisions of Campo Formio, and went farther. It confirmed the annexation of Belgium to France, and the suppression of the ecclesiastical principalities of Germany, thus opening the way to that momentous and final Diet in 1803 which destroyed so many little German States, and rearranged so many local frontiers, that the Holy Roman Empire really came to an end. Lastly among the great Napoleonic treaties comes Tilsit (7 July 1807, France and Russia; 9 July, France and Prussia). By this peace Prussia lost all her territories to the west of the Elbe; and her Polish territories (including Warsaw, annexed in 1795) were reconstituted as an independent Poland under the name of the Duchy of Warsaw.

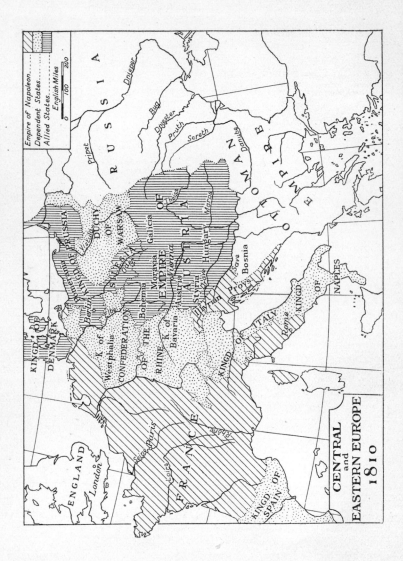

CENTRAL
and
EASTERN EUROPE
1810

Empire of Napoleon........
Dependent States........
Allied States........

English Miles
0   100   200

In 1810, actually annexed to France, administered by French *préfets* and garrisoned by French troops, were Belgium, Holland, and North Germany from the Dutch frontier to Hamburg and Lübeck (except the kingdom of Westphalia under Jerome Bonaparte) ; in southern Europe Piedmont, Genoa, Tuscany, and Rome were now part of France, as were also Carinthia, Istria, Croatia, Carniola, and Dalmatia. So much was actually French territory. In addition, Spain was under King Joseph Bonaparte ; while those parts of Italy which had not been actually annexed were divided between two client kingdoms of the French Empire— the kingdom of Italy under Bonaparte's infant son, and the kingdom of Naples under Joachim Murat. Similarly all Germany outside the line of French occupation, with the exception of a much truncated Prussia and Austria, was grouped in a so-called Confederation of the Rhine (which included even Saxony) wholly dependent on Napoleon : equally dependent was the temporarily revived Poland—the Duchy of Warsaw as it was called—with the King of Saxony as duke.

Undoubtedly European dominion by one Power means Europe in fetters. This was the idea behind the persistent opposition of England to Napoleon ; it was the idea which inspired the ceaseless anti-Napoleonic propaganda of the publicists Pilat and Gentz. The Napoleonic 'Continental System' was itself a gigantic, carefully thought-out scheme for the enslavement of Europe. By the Decree which Napoleon issued from Berlin on the 21st November 1806, no trade was to be allowed between Great Britain and any port of France or of the territory of the allies of France. Every Continental State except Turkey was considered to be an ally, and for a time (with the exception of Turkey and Portugal) accepted the Decree. In the end the Continental System broke down : it was impossible for Napoleon to stop all the gaps by which trade could be carried on with the British Empire ; and the attempt to enforce the blockade throughout

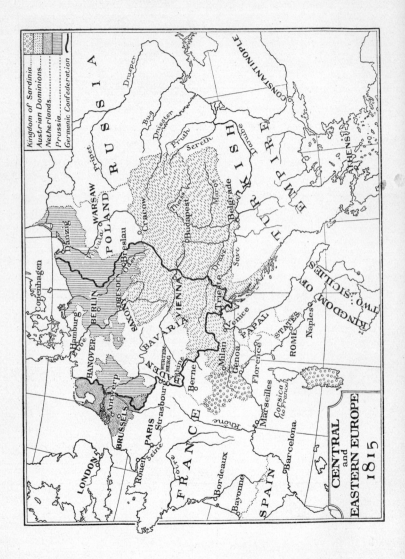

CENTRAL and
EASTERN EUROPE
1815

Kingdom of Sardinia
Austrian Dominions
Netherlands
Prussia
Germanic Confederation

Europe helped to promote that national and popular opposition which culminated in the War of Liberation of 1812–13. Yet no one can say how nearly Napoleon had come to making all Europe as completely one regulated Empire as it had been in the time of Augustus. Such a unified Europe may come again, for the good of the world, but it must come by a free association of States, not by pressure from the mailed heel of a conqueror. The European System of sovereign States is the only possible stage to a Confederation of Europe : and therefore to preserve this European System against a military dominion is a service to humanity. The steady refusal of England to recognize the Napoleonic Empire, her inflexible policy of war against it, were the work of William Pitt and his school of statesmen, who had to deal with a war-weary people, and an eloquent parliamentary peace-party. The temptation is tremendous for the statesmen, who keep the armies at war, to say Peace ! when the prospect in front of them is only years of war with failing allies : but the real sentiment of humanity, the highest courage, the deepest faith, are with those black-coated civilians who say, Fight on ! Oxenstierna in the Thirty Years War, William III in the wars of Louis XIV, Pitt (followed by Castlereagh) in the Napoleonic, Lloyd George in the war of 1914–18, had the vision and the will to save the European System.

VI

The Concert of Europe, 1815–56

§ 1

THE Napoleonic Wars came to an end with two groups of treaties signed between the Allied Powers on the one hand and France on the other, in May 1814, and November 1815. Yet these groups of treaties, known as the First and Second Peace of Paris, could only conclude the state of war and settle the French frontiers : but the rest of Europe had been so cut about by Napoleon, that something more than the cessation of war was required : State territories must be re-defined, and European frontiers must be re-drawn. This was the task of the Congress of Vienna, September 1814 to July 1815. It was not a peace congress : peace had been made at Paris ; it was an assemblage of statesmen to reconstruct the States System of Europe after its ruin by Napoleon. This object was stated in No. 1 of the Separate and Secret Articles of the First Peace of Paris, 30th May 1814.

> The disposal of the Territories given up by his Most Christian Majesty, . . . and the relations from whence a real and permanent Balance of Power in Europe is to be derived, shall be regulated at the Congress upon the principles determined upon by the Allied Powers among themselves. . . .

The statesmen of the Vienna Congress were trying to make an arrangement of Europe which would tend to prevent another great war, and which would be fair to those who had suffered in the last gigantic struggle.

On the whole they did their work well. They re-established the European System of States, and this settlement lasted (with, it is true, considerable modifications) without any general war till 1914. The Treaties of 1815 have not been permanent : almost every decade of the nineteenth century brought some change to them. No one ever meant in 1815 to put Europe into a cast-iron system, but only into one which would be subject to orderly development, not to catastrophic revolution. 'The treaty', said Gentz, in summarizing the results of the Congress, 'has the incontestable merit of having facilitated the way for a more perfect constitution.'

Not that the Congress accomplished everything that its promoters hoped to accomplish. There was too much egotism among the statesmen—an inevitable result of a war waged at such cost : every member of the Congress felt that he must do his best to get compensation to his country for sacrifices suffered. Moreover, France, in the person of Talleyrand, was admitted to the Congress, and Talleyrand was swift to take advantage of any dissensions among the Allies, and to play upon their prejudices, so that France actually exercised great influence on the reconstruction of Europe. Although the Congress nearly split over the compensation terms, and at one time divided itself into two camps which threatened to fight each other, in the end sane counsels prevailed, and the European System of States was peacefully re-established.

The Congress—which in practice consisted only of the five Great Powers, England, Russia, Prussia, Austria, and France—looked at its task from the aspect of ' Restoration ', that is, restoration of the international system which Napoleon had destroyed. But much had been done in the wars which could not be undone. In particular, the mediaeval empire had been abolished and Germany now had no head. On the other hand, its political geography had been simplified : instead of about three hundred and fifty sovereign German States, there were now only thirty-nine. The rest had been suppressed in the Napoleonic period. The Congress of Vienna made no attempt to revive them ; but the existing thirty-nine were made into a Confederation, with a central Diet or Assembly (at Frankfort) and with a perpetual President, Austria. In Italy, on the other hand, most of the old States were restored : the Pope recovered his Temporal Power intact, the kingdom of Naples, the Grand Duchy of Tuscany, the Duchies of Parma and Modena, were all re-established : but the former republics of Genoa and Venice were not : Genoa was added to the kingdom of Sardinia, while Venice and Dalmatia went to Austria, who also recovered her former province of Lombardy.

The danger-spot of the European System of States has always been the Low Countries ; in the eighteenth century Austria had held Belgium, but had never been very successful in maintaining that country's neutrality. So at Vienna Belgium and Holland were joined together, in the hope that they would form one solid State, able to protect the mouths of the Scheldt and the Rhine. Equally statesmanlike, and more practically successful, was the Congress policy towards Switzerland : the ancient Swiss Confederation was re-established with larger territories, and its independence and integrity were given a European guarantee. In eastern Europe, however, a return could not be made to the pre-Revolutionary days. Austria, Russia, and Prussia would not permit the restoration of the Polish State.

In spite of imperfections, the work of the Congress of Vienna was great and enduring. Three things in especial stood forth for all time : the existence of independent, neutral Switzerland, an island of peace and good relations : the freedom of ' international ' rivers ; and the declaration of the Powers against the slave trade. Finally the Congress stood for the only principle by which international relations can be conducted—the principle of good faith : it upheld, with necessary concessions to the facts of the day, the rights of property and the sanctity of contracts.

It is true that Gentz (the General Secretary of the Congress) comments on the egotism and greed of the Powers at Vienna :

> The real purpose of the Congress was to divide amongst the conquerors the spoils taken from the vanquished. (Mem. in Metternich, *Memoirs*, Engl. trans., ii. 553.)

Gentz is hard on the Congress statesmen, except his own master, Metternich, and Castlereagh who, he says, was ' guided by the purest intentions ' (*ibid.*, p. 559). Yet this cynical though sagacious diplomist elsewhere does justice to the work of the Congress of Vienna :

> It is filled with imperfections and *lacunae*. . . . It has the look of a provisional arrangement rather than of a work destined to last for centuries. Nevertheless, after having been severe, it is necessary also to be just. The Treaty, such as it is, has the

incontestable merit of having facilitated the way towards a more perfect political constitution. . . . A large number of troublesome details, of difficult questions, of contradictory pretentions, of thorny arrangements, have now been surmounted. . . . The Treaty has cleared the *terrain* on which it will be possible later to raise a better social edifice. (*Dépêches inédites du Chevalier de Gentz*, i. 169.)

§ 2

During the four years after the Congress of Vienna there was a real Concert of Europe. The idea that the States of Europe were, or might become, a brotherhood for the maintenance of peace was in the minds of many people :

The problem of a universal Alliance for the peace and happiness of the world has always been one of speculation and of hope, but it has never yet been reduced to practice, and if an opinion may be hazarded from its difficulty, it never can ; but you may in practice approach towards it, and perhaps the design has never been so far realized as in the last four years. (Mem. of the British Plenipotentiaries at the Conference of Aix-la-Chapelle, 1818, in Webster, *Congress of Vienna*, pp. 166–71.)

Such was the opinion, on the whole encouraging, of the British Foreign Office concerning the years after the Congress of Vienna. There was again a European States System, and a Concert to attend to its interests. For this fine result, the Foreign Office gave the credit to the Tsar Alexander I of Russia, the designer of the Holy Alliance :

The benign principles of the Alliance of 26th September 1815, having been either formally or substantially adhered to by all Powers, may be considered as constituting the European System in matters of political conscience. (*Ibid.*)

This Holy Alliance, which has in later years met with so much opprobrium, was a declaration of good will between the sovereigns of Russia, Austria, and Prussia :

Conformably to the words of the Holy Scriptures, which command all men to consider each other as brethren, the Three Contracting Monarchs will remain united by the bonds of a true and indissoluble fraternity, and considering each other as fellow-countrymen, they will, on all occasions, and in all places, lend each other aid and assistance ; and regarding themselves towards their subjects and armies, as fathers of families, they will lead them in the same spirit of fraternity with which they are animated, to protect Religion, Peace, and Justice. (Treaty between Russia, Austria, and Prussia, signed at Paris, 26 September 1815.)

This Holy Alliance, excellent in theory, was either too vague, or too narrow for the political needs of Europe : too vague, because all Governments profess to act on Christian, fraternal principles ; too narrow, because, when translated into practice, the Holy Alliance was apt to take the form of interfering in the domestic concerns of independent States.   More practically workable was Castlereagh's plan for a Quadruple Alliance of the chief Powers who had won the war against Napoleon—an alliance with the specific object of seeing that the conditions of the Peace Treaty should be observed.   This limited alliance was made at Paris (as was also the Holy Alliance), on 20th November 1815, at the end of the ' Hundred Days ' :

Art. I.   The High Contracting Parties reciprocally promise to maintain, in its full force and vigour, the Treaty signed this day with His Most Christian Majesty, and to see that the stipulations of the said Treaty . . . shall be strictly and faithfully executed in their fullest extent.

.   .   .   .

Art. VI.   To facilitate and to secure the execution of the present Treaty, and to consolidate the connexions which at the present moment so closely unite the Four Sovereigns for the happiness of the world, the High Contracting Parties have agreed to renew their Meetings at fixed periods, either under the immediate auspices of the Sovereigns themselves or by their respective Ministers, for the purpose of consulting upon their common interests, and for the consideration of the measures which at each of these periods shall be considered the most salutary for the repose and prosperity of Nations, and for the maintenance of the Peace of Europe. (Treaty between Great Britain, Austria, Prussia, Russia, signed at Paris, 20 November 1815.)

Thus, acting under the terms of this Quadruple Alliance, the statesmen of Europe, after the Napoleonic War, met in conference from time to time, to discuss the affairs of Europe, and in especial to prevent causes of renewed war, just as their successors did after the war of 1914–18. For a few years ' Diplomacy by Conference ' became the order of the day ; matters were too urgent, international crises were too imminent, to be settled by exchanges of notes between the Chancelleries. So the high statesmen themselves met, and carried on their discussions in conference.

These conferences were not very numerous. The first—that of Aix-la-Chapelle—occurred in 1818, three years after Waterloo and the Congress of Vienna. France was able to make arrangements with the assistance of the house of Baring, to pay off the war indemnity one year before the specified time. Accordingly the Powers at Aix-la-Chapelle, recognized that

the French Government has fulfilled, with the most scrupulous and honourable punctuality, all the clauses of the Treaties and Conventions of the 20th of November. . . .

The undersigned . . . invite his Excellency [the Duke of Richelieu, Prime Minister of France] to take part in their present and future deliberations, consecrated to the maintenance of the peace, the treaties on which it is founded, the rights and mutual relations established or confirmed by these treaties, and recognized by all the European Powers. (Note addressed by the Plenipotentiaries of Great Britain, Austria, Prussia, and Russia to the Duke of Richelieu, Aix-la-Chapelle, 4 November 1818.)

Thus France, lately the enemy of the States of Europe, was admitted to the Concert.

The next Congress met at Troppau (1820), in Austrian Silesia, to consider the European situation in the light of revolutions which had occurred in the kingdoms of Naples and Spain. With England dissenting (France assented with certain reservations), the Powers asserted the right of intervention in revolutionary States : they claimed to have the right and duty to employ

> peaceful or coercive measures which, in cases where important effects of a salutary influence could be obtained, might recall those States within the bosom of the Alliance.
>
> .   .   .   .
>
> The exercise of this right became still more urgent, when those who had placed themselves in that position [i.e. Revolution] sought to communicate to neighbouring States the misfortune in which they had themselves plunged, and to propagate revolution and confusion around them. (Circular of the Austrian, Russian, and Prussian sovereigns, Troppau, 8 December 1820.)

Acting on this assertion, an Austrian army suppressed the Neapolitan revolution. Two years later a Congress met at Verona further to consider the Spanish trouble. The English representative, the Duke of Wellington, attended only as an onlooker. The result of this Congress was that a French army passed the Pyrenees and suppressed the Spanish Revolution. It was even expected that French, and perhaps Russian, troops would be embarked for South America, to crush the revolutionary movements in the Spanish colonies. The British Government, with George Canning at the Foreign Office, thought that this would be an unwarranted interference with the aspirations of people to settle their own destinies, and proceeded to recognize the independence of the colonies. The Government of the United States took the same view, stimulated in addition by the alarming prospect of French and Russian soldiers on the American Continent. It was for this reason that President Monroe sent his now famous message to Congress, for all the world to read (2 December 1823).

In the wars of the European Powers, in matters relating

to themselves, we have never taken any part, nor does it comport with our policy so to do. It is only when our rights are invaded, or seriously menaced, that we resent injuries, or make preparation for our defence. With the movements of this Hemisphere, we are, of necessity, more immediately connected, and by causes which must be obvious to all enlightened and impartial observers. . . . We owe it, therefore, to candour, and to the amicable relations existing between the United States and those Powers, to declare that we should consider any attempt on their part, to extend their system to any portion of this Hemisphere, as dangerous to our peace and safety. With the existing Colonies or Dependencies of any European Power we have not interfered, and we shall not interfere. But with the Governments who have declared their independence, and maintained it, and whose independence we have, on great consideration, and on just principles acknowledged, we could not view any interposition, for the purpose of oppressing them, or controlling, in any manner, their destiny, by any European Power, in any other light than as the manifestation of an unfriendly disposition towards the United States.

The announcement was sufficient. No French or Russian troops came ; and the South American colonies won their freedom in war with the troops of Old Spain.

Thus America stepped into a position of close relation to the European System, even while proclaiming her isolation from it. Canning took an exaggerated pride in his part :

I sought materials of compensation in another hemisphere. . . . I resolved that if France had Spain, it should not be Spain with the Indies. I called the New World into existence to redress the balance of the old. (Speech in House of Commons, 1823.)

§ 3

With the Congress of Verona of 1822 the ' Congress Period ' came to an end. The sovereigns and high ministers of State no longer met, as it were automatically, to discuss any new matter in connexion with the settlement of 1815. Nevertheless the fruitful idea of the Concert went onwards. The western, central, and eastern States of Europe now regarded themselves as a society of nations, as the guardians of European peace and civilization. In spite of their natural jealousies and conflicting aims, they recognized a common responsibility ; and although they had no stated or regular meetings, they did meet, in partial concert at least, from time to time. The five great Powers usually had a discussion, in a meeting arranged by one or other commanding personality among their ministers, at every great crisis from 1822 to 1856. Then the Crimean War interrupted the Concert ; it was re-established in 1867, but never became so strong as it had been in the years after 1815.

Greece, Belgium, Egypt, and Spain provided the crises which chiefly troubled international relations from the Congress of Verona till the Crimean War. Besides these, there were domestic questions among the Great Powers themselves, disturbing the quiet surface over which Metternich and his friends so anxiously watched. These questions centred round the demand of many Germans for something in the nature of constitutional government. The organic Act of the Germanic Confederation, which the Treaty of Vienna declared to have ' the same force and validity as if textually inserted therein ', promised to all German States separate Assemblies (Art. 13, 8 June 1815). This promise, however, was not carried into effect, as the German statesmen, headed by Metternich, feared that the summoning of parliamentary assemblies might have an effect comparable to that of the meeting of the French Estates General in 1789. This attitude on the part of Metternich really made for European unrest ; parliamentary assemblies help to remove the causes of revolution in three ways : first, by legislating, they enable constitutional changes to be made gradually and peacefully instead of by violence and tumult ; secondly they provide independent criticism of the country's administration, and so prevent abuses which might provoke insurrection ; thirdly they give people the opportunity of stating their views, so that even the most fanatical opinions are submitted to the modifying influence of open discussion, instead of poisoning the subterranean political atmosphere. Thus Metternich, by his extreme nervousness, by his rigid antipathy towards representative assemblies, really helped to produce the revolutionary outbursts of 1848. Indeed, he had little power for good in international affairs after 1822. The leading part was taken by the British Government which believed in parliamentary institutions, and also in the European Concert. The French governing classes on the whole shared these views, so that France and Great Britain gradually came to act together, and the famous (though chequered) *entente* of 1830–56 was formed.

§ 4

The revolt of the Greeks against their Turkish masters began in 1821, and for years the Morea was the scene of a devastating war. It is a characteristic of the European System that when any region is given up to fighting, all the States feel some of the effects of the war, even if it does not spread and become a conflagration. Happily the Greek War of Independence was localized. It lasted for eight years. The efforts of the Powers to bring it to an end were for long ineffective, partly on account of the natural unwillingness of the Sultan Mahmud to agree to the suggestions of Europe, partly because the Powers of Europe did not all desire the same thing. The British, French, and Russian Governments did, however, work to a certain extent in concert. They agreed by treaty that Greece should be autonomous, and that they should combine to urge both Greek and Turk to accept an armistice (Treaty of London, 6 July 1827). The Greeks accepted the armistice but the Porte (not unnaturally, for the military situation was favourable to it) refused ; friction arose between the Turkish and western forces ; and the naval action of

Navarino (October 1827) went a long way towards ending the long struggle. The final settlement was made in a series of conferences at Constantinople and London between 1829 and 1832 : on the 21th July 1832 the Plenipotentiaries of Great Britain, France, and Russia at the Turkish capital were able to declare in their last Protocol : ' the Greek Question is irrevocably settled.' This statement was true: under the guidance of the Three Powers, Greece had become irrevocably free. Subsequent changes were only normal developments of this principle.

After Greece, came Belgium. This country, formerly under Austrian rule, had been united to Holland by Article 65 of the Vienna Congress Act. In July 1830 there was a peaceful revolution in Paris ; Charles X had to give place to his more constitutionally inclined cousin Louis-Philippe. The Paris *coup d'état* acted like a spark to a powder magazine in Belgium : the country rose against the union with Holland. Here there was the first really serious menace to the States System of Europe as established by the Congress of Vienna. The Great Powers had carefully constructed a compact and strong State, holding the mouths of the Scheldt and the Rhine, and keeping France and Germany apart : and now this compact State was being split into two. No wonder that the guardians of European peace were nervous. They would have preferred that Belgium should stay with Holland, but she refused to do so. A free union was impossible : and the Powers had no intention of trying to preserve a forced union for ever. So they met in London—the plenipotentiaries of Great Britain, Austria, France, Prussia, and Russia—and agreed that Belgium should be free and independent. In addition, in order to safeguard that danger-spot of Europe, they decided that Belgium's territory should be neutral and inviolate (Treaty of London, 15 November 1831). It took nearly eight years before the kingdom of Holland would recognize this new condition of affairs ; but at last it consented to be persuaded in a new Conference ; and

Belgium, with the territories and international status which were hers for the next eighty years, obtained complete recognition

GREECE
1832–1913
English Miles
0   50   100
Greek frontiers 1913 ⎯⎯⎯
    „   „   1881 ⎯⎯⎯
    „   „   1832 ....

in the celebrated Treaty of London, on the 19th April 1839. Article 7 of the Annex to this Treaty (the Annex having the same force as the Treaty itself) declared that 'Belgium within the limits specified . . . shall form an Independent and perpetually

Neutral State. It shall be bound to observe such Neutrality towards all other States '.

The Vienna Settlement was thus amended by consent of all interested parties : the organization of the States System was modified, but not destroyed : in fact, it stood better than ever, through the admission to the System of a prosperous, peaceful, and legally minded new State, such as Belgium has proved herself to be.

§ 5

As the nineteenth century went on, the Eastern Question, which had been left out of consideration at the Congress of Vienna, became more insistent. Gradually the Powers came to realize that Constantinople was a vital point in the European System. The Eastern Question really meant—what was to be done with Constantinople ? The gaining of their freedom by the Serbs in 1815 and by the Greeks in 1821–9 had demonstrated to Europe that Turkey would probably have to lose, one by one, her Christian provinces : but the ultimate question still remained : what was to be done with Constantinople ?

The Russian Government had its answer ready. When in 1832 Mehemet Ali, Pasha of Egypt, sent his son Ibrahim to fight against his master the Sultan, and when Ibrahim scattered the Turkish forces at Konia (21 December 1832), the Porte, to save the capital, appealed for aid. Even before the battle Turkey had invited British support and had been refused. So the Sultan turned to Russia : help was quickly furnished, and a Russian fleet anchored in the Bosphorus. But the Porte had to pay dearly for Russian help. By the Treaty of Unkiar Skelessi, on 8th July 1833, the two States made a defensive alliance. The Tsar promised military help in time of need : in return

the Sublime Ottoman Porte, in place of the aid which it is bound to furnish in case of need . . . shall confine its action in favour of the Imperial Court of Russia to closing the Strait

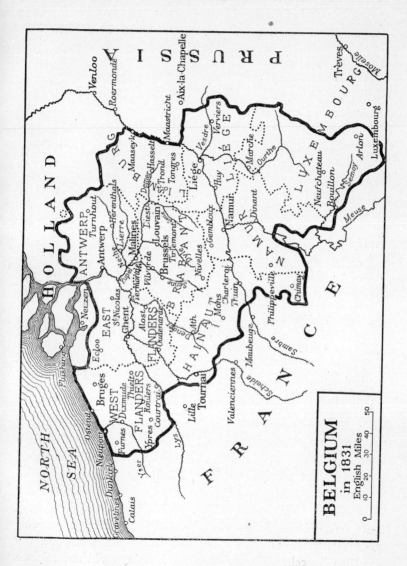

BELGIUM
in 1831
English Miles

0 10 20 30 40 50

of the Dardanelles, that is to say, to not allowing any foreign vessels of war to enter therein under any pretext whatsoever. (Secret Article.)

Russian warships could go through the Strait : no others could do so. Thus Turkey became, on paper, a military protectorate enfeoffed to the Tsar. This was one way of settling the Eastern Question.

Stratford Canning, the most eminent of the diplomatists who have held the English embassy at Constantinople, had already warned the British Government of the danger of inaction. On 19 December 1832 (before the battle of Konia, and six months before the Treaty of Unkiar Skelessi) he had written :

> The Turkish Empire has reached, in its decline, that critical point at which it must either revive and commence a fresh era of prosperity, or fall into a state of complete dissolution. To Great Britain the fate of this Empire can never be indifferent. It would affect the interests of her trade and East Indian possessions, even if it were unconnected with the maintenance of her relative power in Europe. . . .
>
> That Empire [the Turkish Empire] may fall to pieces at all events ; and he must be a bold man who would undertake to answer for its being saved by any effort of human policy. But His Majesty's Government may rest assured that to leave it to itself is to leave it to its enemies. (Foreign Office, 'Turkey', 211, 19 December 1832.)

Too late Lord Palmerston realized the truth of Stratford Canning's warning. He had left Turkey to her enemy Russia, who thereupon proceeded to reduce her to the position of a client State by the Treaty of Unkiar Skelessi. But Palmerston was resolved to rectify his mistake. Luck favoured him. When in 1839 Mehemet Ali again attacked the Turkish Empire, and won (through Ibrahim) the great battle of Nisib, Palmerston let Count Nesselrode, the Russian Chancellor, know that Great Britain would not tolerate any single-handed intervention on the part of Russia. The

French Government, equally anxious to prevent the Tsar from engulfing Turkey, openly sided with Great Britain : and Austria and Prussia showed no tendency to break a lance for their former 'Holy Ally'. Faced with this spectacle of unanimity on the part of the Central and Western Powers, the Tsar behaved with wisdom and with moderation. He waived his rights under the Treaty of Unkiar Skelessi, and joined the Concert of the Powers to settle in amicable discussion the affairs of Turkey and Mehemet Ali. The task of the Powers was not easy, and before it was concluded Great Britain and France lost their accord, and all but came to blows. But the war cloud blew over, and in a Conference over which Palmerston presided at London in the summer of 1841, the 'Convention of the Straits' was drafted and signed by the Five Great Powers and the Porte. The Sultan was made the Guardian of the Dardanelles and Bosphorus, and was bound to exclude all foreign ships of war, so long as he himself was at peace.

> So long as the Porte is at peace, His Highness will admit no Foreign Ship of War into the said Straits. (Treaty of London, 13 July 1841.)

Thus the structure known as the States System of Europe was cemented at that vital part in the south-east of the Continent, where Constantinople makes a bridge between Europe and Asia, and links Russia with the West.

§ 6

Although the Tsar Nicholas I had yielded to the Concert in 1840–1, he was not always prepared to do so. For years the power of Russia had been growing : never did her prestige stand so high as under Alexander I, and his brother and successor Nicholas. The colossal Empire of the Tsar broke the Vienna Congress Act, and the Western Powers dared not say it nay. In 1830 the

'Congress Kingdom' of Poland (of which the Tsar was King) was suppressed: and in 1846 a Russo-Prusso-Austrian Treaty allowed Austria to annex the Free City of Cracow. Thus the first and sixth Articles of the Vienna Congress Treaty were violated by three of the signatories without any reference to the other Signing Powers: Lord Palmerston protested that

> it is not competent for 3 of those Powers by their own separate authority to undo that which was established by the common engagements of the whole: and it is manifest that the special duty which the 3 Powers undertook, of protecting the Independence of the State [Cracow] cannot invest them with any right to overthrow that independence and to destroy it.

This last sentence is a pointed observation which shows the difficulties under which statesmen laboured, who were striving to maintain the European System: some of its very defenders were the people who from time to time conspired against it.

The bonds of European cohesion were growing weaker, when in 1848 revolutions in France, Italy, Prussia, and Austria seemed to throw the System into chaos. The Austrian Empire, so useful as a guarantor of peace among the jealous races of south-central Europe, now went into the pangs of dissolution; but the Empire of the young Francis Joseph was marvellously saved and restored to strength by the skill and steadfastness of Schwarzenberg (the chancellor who had succeeded Metternich), by the military skill of Radetzky and Windischgrätz, and by the help of the army of the Tsar Nicholas I. Never, since King John Sobieski saved Vienna in 1683, had one sovereign rendered such signal service to another. Austria had reason to be grateful: but 'some day' said Schwarzenberg, 'we shall astonish the world by our ingratitude'. These words came true in the year after this great chancellor's death.

Russia maintained her high position in the eye of Europe until the Crimean War. This struggle, which has since been the subject of much misunderstanding, arose out of the apprehensions which the Western Powers felt of the Tsar's ambitions. There is no doubt that Nicholas I had designs upon the independence of Turkey. The celebrated Hamilton Seymour conversations (published as a parliamentary paper after the war had started) prove this. Seymour was ambassador at St. Petersburg in the years preceding the war. In January–February 1853 the Tsar favoured him with interviews, during which he made the now famous allusion to Turkey as the sick man, and offered to come to an understanding with England for a scheme of partition of the Ottoman dominions. Therefore, when the Tsar publicly pressed the claims of the Greek monks in Bethlehem against the Latin monks, and when he himself claimed the right to 'protect' subjects of Turkey who worshipped according to the Greek rite, he was merely giving indications of a wider scheme for the control of Turkey, schemes of which the British Foreign Office had evidence in its archives.

The Crimean War was therefore fought on the part of Great Britain and France in order to vindicate the place of Turkey as a part of the European States System. It is solely from this point of view that the war must be judged. If Turkey was not to be part of the European States System what alternative remained ? None of the Balkan States at that time could have stepped into the place of Turkey. The only possible successor to the Sultan in the middle of the nineteenth century was the Tsar. But if the Tsar gained Constantinople and the Straits he would, sooner or later, become one of those 'disturbers' of Europe, one of those all-but dominators, who have always met, and always must meet, a European coalition and war on a European scale. The Crimean War was a more limited struggle, war on the grand, though not on the European, scale, and it prevented the rise of Russia as a disturber or dominator of the Continent. This fact was at the back of the minds of the British, and probably of the French, public. It explains the enthusiasm

shown for the war : the war was felt to be against a colossus,
which stood for domination and political reaction :

> And as months ran on and rumour of battle grew,
> ' It is time, it is time, O passionate heart,' said I
> (For I cleaved to a cause that I felt to be pure and true),
> ' It is time, O passionate heart and morbid eye,
> That old hysterical mock-disease should die.'
> And I stood on a giant deck and mixed my breath
> With a loyal people shouting a battle-cry,
> Till I saw the dreary phantom arise and fly
> Far into the North, and battle, and seas of death.
> Let it go or stay, so I wake to the higher aims
> Of a land that has lost for a little her lust of gold,
> And love of a peace that was full of wrongs and shames,
> Horrible, hateful, monstrous, not to be told ;
> And hail once more to the banner of battle unroll'd !
>
> (Tennyson, *Maud.*)

The intervention of Sardinia in the war, on the side of France
and Great Britain, must not be ascribed to merely ' nationalist '
causes. Cavour desired to unite Italy : but he also desired Italy
to be a Power, to be recognized as a normal and wholesome
member of the European System. So, as Sardinia had done in
the time of Louis XIV and Bonaparte, she now entered the war
against the disturber of Europe. She gained her reward almost
immediately. At the Congress of Paris in 1856, at the end of the
Crimean War, Sardinia sat as one of the Powers, and discussed
and took part in decisions concerning international relations in
Europe and in the whole world.

The Congress of Paris cannot perhaps rank with the Congress
of Westphalia, of Vienna, or of Versailles ; yet it stands out in
the history of the European System because it definitely adopted
Turkey as part of that System :

> H.M. the Queen, the United Kingdom of Great Britain and
> Ireland, H.M. the Emperor of Austria, . . . France, . . . Russia,
> H.M. the King of Prussia, . . . of Sardinia, declare the Sublime

Porte admitted to participate in the advantages of the Public Law and System of Europe (*à participer aux avantages du droit public et du concert européen*). (Article VII of the Treaty of Paris, 30 March 1856.)

In the same article the Powers guaranteed in common the independence and integrity of Turkey. The Sultan was again recognized as the guardian of the Straits, and to strengthen his position *vis-à-vis* Russia, the whole Black Sea was neutralized: there were to be neither Turkish nor Russian fortifications on its shores, nor warships on its waters.

The Treaty of Paris gave to Turkey a definite place and a strong position in the European System. On the whole she maintained this place adequately, in spite of internal mal-administration, and in spite of the deplorable massacres of Christian subjects which greatly injured her in international public opinion. Yet when really tested in a more than usually severe crisis, she broke down. Had Turkey remained neutral in the War of 1914, and loyally fulfilled her function as Guardian of the Straits (excluding ships of war of all nations), she would have vindicated her position at Constantinople and in the European States System for all time.

Besides dealing with the position of Turkey in the system, the Congress of Paris took steps to define the law of the sea in time of war. The demands which had so often been made on the British Admiralty were now, with necessary reservations, conceded by the British Government: and something—the rule of blockade— was granted to the British point of view:

1. Privateering is, and remains, abolished.
2. The Neutral Flag covers Enemy's Goods, with the exception of Contraband of War.
3. Neutral Goods, with the exception of Contraband of War, are not liable to capture under Enemy's Flag.
4. Blockades, in order to be binding, must be effective, that is to say, maintained by a force sufficient really to prevent access to the coast of the enemy.

These rules have never been officially declared to be suppressed although they broke down in the European War of 1914–18.

With the question of Constantinople settled, with the law of the sea defined, with Russia, Austria, Prussia, Great Britain, and Sardinia all united in Congress, it may be claimed that in 1856 Europe was a real System of States. To make the system a real thing the Congress adopted a Protocol (No. 23), introduced by the Earl of Clarendon :

> The Plenipotentiaries do not hesitate to express, in the name of their Governments, the wish that States between which any serious misunderstanding may arise, should before appealing to Arms, have recourse, as far as circumstances might allow, to the Good Offices of a friendly Power.

Although this Protocol, when invoked by Lord Clarendon in 1866, was unable to prevent the Austro-Prussian War, and when invoked again by the same statesman in 1870, had no effect on the Franco-Prussian crisis of that day, yet it was a potent idea, and has now passed into international law in Article 12 of the League of Nations Covenant.

VII

The System receives new Members

THE most momentous fact in the history of international relations in the last half of the nineteenth century was the entrance of two new members into the European System. Throughout the first half of the nineteenth century there were two areas—in addition to other danger spots—where instability prevailed : these were Italy and Germany. Seven States partitioned Italy, and thirty-nine partitioned Germany. The existence of a large number of minor States in one geographical area gave opportunities for intrigue, both external and internal, and so helped to produce political crises. In Italy, Austria was predominant, and kept the peace, but she was not sufficiently powerful to do so permanently. In Germany, the influence of Austria was declining after 1815, and was continually being thwarted by Prussia. This condition of affairs certainly did not make for peace. The consolidation of Italy into a kingdom and of Germany into an empire gave political stability to those important areas of Europe, and might reasonably have been expected to contribute to the general peace. Indeed it would have done so, had not militarism gained control of German policy during the process of union. The union of Italy, on the other hand, was actually due to diplomacy as much as to arms, and during the course of the movement for union the Italian civilian statesmen never gave away to the soldiers the directing of policy.

Both the union of Italy and the union of Germany were made by breaches in the public law of Europe. The political System of Europe, the external—not the internal—economy of States, had been defined by the General Act of the Congress of Vienna, and the Governments had all subscribed their signatures to this ordinance. But the public law was never meant to be a rigid code, inelastic, unalterable. It was a System designed to meet the existing needs of Europe, and capable of being modified, as occasion arose, to suit those needs. Such changes, however, such adaptations, should be made by the same means as those by which the System had been established, namely, by Conference and by treaties among the constituent States. It was to make such peaceful modifications of the System possible that the European Concert existed.

When during the nineteenth century the sentiment of nationality grew stronger, and aspirations after union became intensified in Italy and Germany, the Governments of Europe contemplated the meeting of Congresses to enable the Italian States (and likewise the German States) to adjust their differences by agreement and by mutual give and take. In England Lord John Russell, in France Napoleon III, were equally insistent upon this plan. As regards Italy, the method of settlement by Conference was not entirely impracticable. The Government of Sardinia was willing to meet Austria across the Conference-table, and to negotiate for the cession of Lombardy and Venetia on the basis of pecuniary compensation to the Habsburgs. But could Austria accept such a proposal ? The proud Habsburgs would not traffic and huckster for their provinces ; and it could scarcely be expected that by a *beau geste* they should give away their Italian provinces, which were all that they had got from the sacrifice of their Belgian and Rhenish possessions in the Napoleonic wars. So, if Austria could not give up Lombardy and Venetia peacefully, there was little for the Concert to do : war must settle the question.

The question of German union was quite different. The existing Germanic Confederation as established by the Congress of Vienna could easily have been modified by Conference. Austria was not particularly attached to her place in the Confederation ; the other German States, with the possible exception of Prussia, had no objection to the continuation of Habsburg pre-eminence. Even the Prussians were not, before 1864, as a whole anti-Austrian. As the history of the Frankfort Parliament of 1848–9 showed, there was plenty of opinion in Germany to make a peaceful readjustment of the Germanic system possible. But the Prussian Junkers would not have this ; and so from first to last, the modern German Empire was the creation of war, without the Concert of Europe being consulted on a single occasion. The public law, so far as it affected Central Europe, was destroyed by violence and a new System was put in its place, without the Concert Powers, who were the makers and guardians of that law, being permitted to co-operate in its remodelling. That is why Central Europe after 1870 became a sort of armed camp. The roots of the modern German Empire were not in the past. It was a *par-venu* in the ancient society of European States. But time would remedy this defect. Unfortunately, the war of 1914 came before the anodyne had been long enough at work.

.   .   .   .

There is always a tendency among those who read or write history to consider that everything which has taken place was always inevitable. Yet in the year 1858 there can have been few people who thought that the little kingdom of Sardinia had much chance of making a union of Italy. In 1848, the year of revolutions, there had seemed to be a better chance : for Milan, Venice, and Rome had all risen in arms, and King Charles Albert of Sardinia was able to start a national war of Italy against the Habsburgs. But the battle of Novara, 23 March 1849, ruined his enterprise. Charles Albert abdicated. The risings in Rome and Venice collapsed. In 1854 the Sardinian Government made an important step in advance when it joined the constitutional Powers, England and France, in the war against Russia. Still, the Austrians had not released their hold on any part of Italy.

In 1858 and 1859 events came thick and fast. The First Minister of Sardinia, Cavour, and the Emperor Napoleon III had an informal meeting at Plombières (21, 22 July 1858). Napoleon promised to help Sardinia, on condition of receiving Nice and Savoy. The British Government worked hard for a Congress, but the Austrian Government, after bearing with patience extreme tension in its Italian dominions and a violent press-campaign outside, at last most unwisely declared war, and so put Sardinia into the condition of a defender. In the hostilities that followed the Franco-Sardinian forces gained the battles of Magenta and Solferino ; and although Napoleon III did not carry out all his promises, he at least gained Lombardy for Sardinia by the Treaty of Villafranca (11 July 1859). Revolutions against the Grand Duke of Tuscany, the Dukes of Parma and Modena, and the

Temporal Power of the Pope, soon added Central Italy (but not Rome itself) to the Sardinian State ; and Garibaldi's filibustering raid (May 1860), owing to the astounding feebleness of the Neapolitan army, brought the annexation to Sardinia of the kingdom of Naples and Sicily. Thus old European thrones toppled to the dust, and the Public Law counted almost as nothing. In 1861 King Victor Emanuel of Sardinia took the title of King of Italy. In 1866, by taking part against Austria in the Austro-Prussian War of that year, he gained Venetia ; and on the 20th September 1870, about six weeks after the opening of the Franco-Prussian War, his troops entered Rome. The Temporal Power of the Papacy disappeared, and all Italy was united under one national prince.

The union of Germany was a long drawn-out affair. Two events especially mark it. The first was the dissolution of the Germanic Confederation. The second was the Franco-Prussian War. The dissolution of the Germanic Confederation, although its Constitution was embodied in the Vienna Congress Act and therefore was part of the Public Law of Europe, was brought about by *force majeure* without reference to the Concert of Europe at all. In 1866 Austria and Prussia quarrelled and fought over the duchies of Schleswig and Holstein, which they had seized from Denmark two years previously. The war only lasted six weeks. Austria was fairly severely defeated and therefore consented, in a bi-lateral treaty with Prussia, that the Germanic Confederation should be dissolved (Treaty of Prague, 23 August 1866). It is impossible, however, to see any lawful ground by which those two members of the European Society of States could dissolve a Confederation for which Europe as a whole was responsible.

In place of the old Confederation, a North German Confederation was established ; of this new organization Austria was not a member ; the King of Prussia was hereditary President : and the territorial boundary was fixed on the south at the river Main.

SAVOY

LOMBARDY

Magenta
Solferino

PIEDMONT

VENETIA

Triest

Lucca

MODENA

ROMAGNA

TUSCANY

Ancona

CORSICA

Rome

UMBRIA

Caprera I

NAPLES

Naples

SARDINIA

Messina

Marsala

SICILY

The
UNION of ITALY
1859-70
English Miles

0   100   200

Piedmont Sardinia in Apr 1859
Added in November 1859
  "   "   "   March 1860
  "   "   "   Oct. & Nov. 1860
  "   "   "   October 1866
  "   "   "   September 1870
Lost in March 1860
Districts claimed by Italy 1914

Bismarck's great work was not yet completed, for Bavaria and the other South-German States were outside the North German Confederation. But they joined in the Franco-Prussian War of 1870 ; and in the national enthusiasm which the success of that war produced they consented to the formation of the German Empire, in the *Galerie des Glaces* at Versailles, on the 18th January 1871. The new Empire included all the German States except Austria, and the King of Prussia was always to be Emperor.

.   .   .   .

By the formation of the united Italian Kingdom, and of the German Empire, two new Great Powers were added to the European System. On the balance, however, Europe only gained one Great Power. The old System had included, as Great States, Great Britain, France, Austria, Prussia, and Russia. Now, however, Prussia had been merged in Germany, or rather Germany had been merged in Prussia ; so that the Great Powers now consisted of Great Britain, France, Austria, Russia, the German Empire, and Italy. Thus the States System was different after 1870 from what it was before. The German Empire was more powerful than the old Prussia had been. Austria, on the other hand, was now less powerful than formerly. · If she had not suffered by her loss of territory, she had suffered in reputation, in confidence, and in self-respect. The entrance of United Italy into the States System was salutary, helping to compensate for the weakening of Austria and for the expansion of Prussia. Great Britain and Russia remained as before. But France was not the same. She had lost Alsace and Lorraine to the new German Empire (Treaty of Versailles, 26 February, and of Frankfort, 10 May 1871), and had thus suffered a moral and material loss which she could not forget. Here was perhaps the weakest point of the European System after 1870. Old boundaries have the stability of long habit. New boundaries have to be kept by the sword. The new boundary of Germany on the west of Alsace

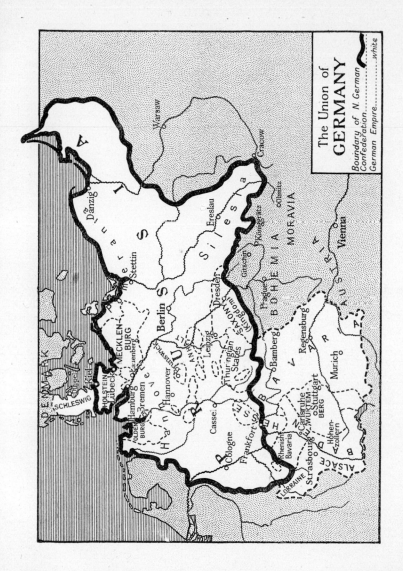

The Union of
GERMANY

Boundary of N. German
Confederation............
German Empire..........white

and Lorraine never became quite habitual in the minds of Europe, but was always a cause of suspicion and friction. This was the mistake of Bismarck and his military friends. Had they not insisted upon the inclusion of Alsace and Lorraine in the new German Empire, that Empire might be with us still, a wholesome member of the Society of European States.

VIII

The European System, 1871–1914

§ 1

THERE is some ground for holding that, except for the wound caused by the annexation of Alsace and Lorraine, and in spite of frequently recurring crises, the European System of States was sound in the years from 1871 to 1914. During that period, the Concert of Europe was a well-understood thing, although it had no constitution and was not established in any specific diplomatic Act or Charter. The Five Great Powers knew that the peace of Europe depended upon them, and whenever international danger was threatened, they deliberately drew together and laboured to construct a bridge over the difficulty. It is impossible to say how many wars the Concert prevented, because no one knows whether things which did not occur might, under other conditions, very easily have occurred. Probably the Concert actually prevented at least seven great European wars.

The first war-crisis which the Concert dissolved took place in the decade previous to the Franco-Prussian War. This was the Luxembourg affair in 1867. The Grand Duchy of Luxembourg had been created by the Congress of Vienna and had been given to the King of Holland. In 1866 and 1867 Napoleon III arranged to buy it from the king, and would have completed the transaction but for the opposition of Prussia. But France could not with dignity withdraw in face of the Prussian threats; and it appeared that nothing could avert a war. Instead of this, however, Lord Stanley, the British Foreign Secretary, managed to convoke a Conference at London (May 1867), in which the new Kingdom of Italy for the first time figured as a Great Power. The result was that France renounced her bargain to purchase Luxembourg, and that Prussia on her side withdrew the garrison which, under the arrangements of the Vienna Congress, she had the right to keep in Luxembourg city. The Grand Duchy was then taken out of the orbit both of France and of Prussia by being neutralized (Treaty between Great Britain, Austria, France, Prussia, Russia, Italy, Belgium, and the Netherlands, signed at London, 11 May 1867).

After the Franco-Prussian War and the creation of the German Empire there was another war-crisis. Bismarck was always nervous about the provinces of Alsace and Lorraine, and was very apprehensive of the revival of French military strength. In 1875 he affected to take umbrage at French criticism of Imperial Germany's clerical policy, and he also suddenly expressed grave doubts about France's policy towards Belgian neutrality; so he presented certain demands to the French Government—demands which seemed bound to provoke France, most unwillingly, into war. For a few weeks hostilities appeared to be inevitable; but they were avoided, not by a meeting of the Concert, but by advice tendered to Bismarck by the British, and more particularly by the Russian, Governments. Thus, although no Congress was assembled, the opinion against war, which prevailed in the Chancelleries of the Great Powers, was sufficient to prevent it.

In the summer of 1878, at the end of the war in which Russia had defeated the Turkish armies, and when Russian soldiers were encamped along the shore within ten miles of Constantinople, a European war over the partition of Turkey was certainly possible, and all too likely. The British fleet was lying outside the Dardanelles ; and the published correspondence between Queen Victoria and Lord Beaconsfield shows that the British Government at least did not shrink from the contest. Austria, Italy, and Greece were all vitally interested. Everything was ready for a great catastrophe. That the European peace was not broken was due in large part to the moderation and self-restraint of the Russian Government which, in deference to the arguments of Great Britain, agreed to modify the Russo-Turkish Treaty of San Stefano (3 March 1878)—the Treaty which had so offended the British policy. But even then there were plenty of chances left for a European war to break forth. These chances, however, were avoided by the Congress of Berlin which, under the presidency of Bismarck, sat from the 13th June to the 13th July. The Treaty of Berlin, though subsequently gashed in many places, remained in its essentials, regulating the political map of the Balkans, until the year 1912.

By Article 1, the Treaty of Berlin set up Bulgaria as an autonomous Principality under the suzerainty of the Sultan. The new Principality's territory was limited by the Balkans. To the south of these mountains a province was formed, to be called Eastern Rumelia, under a Christian Governor-General (it was united after a *coup d'état* in Philippopolis to Bulgaria in 1886). Article 23 promised Organic Laws to the Ottoman territories in Europe. By Article 25 Bosnia and Herzegovina were to be occupied and administered by Austria-Hungary. Serbia, Montenegro, and Rumania all had their independence recognized and their territories increased, although Montenegro, while given a seaport, was not allowed to have any ships of war (Article 29). The European Commission was maintained in being for the regulation and administration of the lower Danube (Article 53). Religious liberty was to be observed both in the Balkan States and throughout the Ottoman Empire.

A fourth crisis, which had all the elements necessary for producing a grand 'succession' war, was averted in 1885 by the Conference of Berlin. This time Africa, in particular tropical Africa, was the bone of contention. All the Great Powers had wakened up to the opportunities for gaining vast tracts of undeveloped territory there. People were talking of a 'scramble' for Africa. The semi-official explorers, and the strong-minded, zealous officials of many nations, were racing to stake out imperial claims. The Conference of Berlin regulated the race, and provided the means for a peaceful partition and for equal opportunities. Its chief work was to declare the great rivers Congo and Niger open to the commerce of all nations, to define *possession*, and to remove a large section of the Dark Continent from the ambitions of the Great Powers by creating the entity which was later known as the Congo Free State.

Early in the twentieth century, in 1905, a very severe crisis took place. The cause this time was the clashing of French and German interests in Morocco. The now celebrated Kühlmann, then Imperial Minister to Morocco, was not the man to allow German interests to be overclouded by the energy of French bankers and diplomatists. Yet neither France nor Germany was looking for war ; and Prince Bülow himself, the Imperial Chancellor, demanded a conference. The Concert met at Algeciras, and by a General Act (7 April 1906) regulated the international position of Morocco.

In 1911 Germany and France again nearly came to blows over Morocco. The incidents which produced the greatest tension were the dispatch of a French military expedition to Fez, and the arrival of a small German warship (the *Panther*) at Agadir. But the war-crisis passed away in the face of Franco-British solidarity, as evinced in the speech of the British Chancellor of the Exchequer, Mr. Lloyd George, at the Guildhall on the 21st July 1911. Although in this case no conference was held, it is fair to claim that the Concert was at work, and that the general desire and effort for peace among the Chancelleries of the Great Powers was effective as well as the vigorous speech of Mr. Lloyd George.

Towards the end of summer, 1912, the Balkan States, which had formed a *League* under the inspiration of Eleutherios Venizelos, presented a note to Turkey demanding the execution (long promised, long delayed) of Article 23 of the Treaty of Berlin. This article stated that 'similar laws [i.e. similar to the Organic Law of 1868 which was to be applied to Crete] . . . shall also be introduced into the other parts of Turkey in Europe'. As the Porte did not assent to the note, a war known as the First Balkan War broke out ; and the allied Balkan States conquered all Turkey in Europe, except the Gallipoli Peninsula and the land behind Chatalja where Constantinople itself is situated. Yet having won the war, the Balkan States were unable to agree upon the division of the conquered territory, although they had previously made certain partition-agreements.

In the summer of 1913 a Conference of Powers, sitting under the Presidency of Sir Edward Grey (Lord Grey of Fallodon) at St. James's, tried to avert a second Balkan War, and appeared to have done so when it negotiated the Treaty of London which the belligerent States of the First Balkan War signed on the 30th May 1913. This Treaty reduced Turkey in Europe to the territory east of a line drawn from Enos on the Aegean to Midia on the Black Sea (Article 2). But when the Treaty had been made, Bulgaria, unable to agree with Serbia and Greece over the division of the ceded Ottoman territory, attacked her allies and so precipitated the Second Balkan War. This was terminated through the military intervention of Rumania, and the Treaty of Bucharest was concluded between Rumania, Greece, Monte-negro, and Serbia (10 August 1913). This treaty left a rankling sore in the Balkans, for Bulgaria had to resign, in favour of Serbia,

BALKAN STATES
1878-1914

English Miles

0   50   100   200

HUNGARY

BUKOVINA

RUSSIA

MOLDAVIA

Jassy

TRANSYLVANIA

BESSARABIA

Temesvar

Rother Turm P.

Galatz

1856-1878

Vulkan P.

Tomos P.

1878

AUSTRIA

BOSNIA

Orsova

Belgrade

WALLACHIA

RUMANIA

Bucharest

DOBRUJA

BLACK SEA

DALMATIA (AUSTRIA)

Serajevo

SERBIA

Silistria

1913

HERZEGOVINA

Vidin

Rustchuk

MONTE NEGRO

Nish

Pirot

Plevna

BULGARIA

Varna

Cattaro

Cettinje

Tirnovo

Sofia

Durazzo

Uskub

1913

1885

Burgas

Philippopolis

1913

ADRIATIC SEA

1913

1913

Adrianople

1913

ITALY

Brindisi

1913

Ochrida

Monastir

Constantinople

OTTOMAN

Valona

1913

Salonica

Otranto

Yanina

AEGEAN SEA

EMPIRE

Corfu

Larissa

1881

Lemnos

J.ROY

IONIAN

Levkas

GREECE

Mitylene

Smyrna

Cephalonia

Chios

SEA

Zante

PELOPONNESUS

Athens

Samos

Crete

Acquisitions of Montenegro 1913

"   "   Roumania   "

"   "   Bulgaria   "

"   "   Serbia   "

"   "   Greece   "

Ceded to Bulgaria by the Treaty
of London May 30th 1913, retroceded
to Turkey Sept 29th 1913

State frontiers _____

Old   "   ....

her claim to Central Macedonia (Uskub) ; and to Rumania (as an indemnity for this State's intervention) she had to cede the Southern Dobruja (Silistria and Balchik). Further, helpless after her exhausting campaigns and without friends, Bulgaria had a few weeks later to retrocede to the Turks her grand conquest of the First Balkan War, Adrianople (Treaty of Constantinople, 29 September 1913). All this may help to explain why the Bulgarian king brooded on revenge for the next two years, and joined in the European War, on the Turco-German side, against Serbia, in October 1915.

The last effort of the European Concert before it expired was to try and deal with the fatal war-crisis of June–July 1914. It is well known that Sir Edward Grey's appeal to Germany for a Conference of the Powers fell on deaf ears (Goschen to Grey, 27 July 1914, in *Collected Diplomatic Documents*, p. 38, No. 43). Yet it is no fair condemnation of the Concert to say that, though it settled many crises, it broke down at last. It had given over forty years of peace.

The persistent effort of a large section of the European public to provide peaceful means for adjusting disputes within the States System was displayed in many ways, especially at the Hague Conferences of 1899 and 1907. At these Conferences all the chief States of the world were represented. Although the grand object for which the Tsar Nicholas II had convoked the Conferences— the limitation of armaments—was not achieved, a notable body of agreements was made for amending the laws and customs relating to war. Some of these agreements became dead letters ; they did not all disappear in the Great War of 1914–18.

The most important decision arrived at by the First Hague Conference (and adhered to by the Second) was to establish a Permanent Court of Arbitration at the Hague. The Court, however, could only act when cases were voluntarily referred to it by the interested parties. By another convention at the Conference of 1907 the chief States of the world agreed not to make war without giving previous and explicit warning. A convention for ameliorating the laws and customs of war was signed by the Conference States ; the chief points in this defined the position and liability of the non-combatant inhabitants of invaded territory, and assured humane treatment of prisoners of war. Article 22 of this convention stated that ' belligerents have not got an unlimited right as to the choice of means of injuring the enemy '. Article 23 then proceeded to forbid the use of poison or poisoned weapons.

§ 2

Until 1914 the Concert of Europe existed but it was not complete. There was a feeling of common responsibility among the Governments of the Great Powers, and there was a habit among them of meeting together when emergencies arose, but all this could not obliterate the grounds, which actually existed, of mutual suspicion. Thus there was a tendency for each Great Power to stand alone and to pursue its own interests. Yet as no Power really could stand alone, and as, on the other hand, the Concert was not sufficiently complete to ensure the safety and interests of each individual State, a middle course between absolute co-operation and individualism in international affairs was adopted : leagues or groups were formed inside the Concert Powers. The first group was the Triple Alliance of 1882. The second was the Triple Entente of 1907.

The terms of the famous *Triplice*, which aroused so much interest and curiosity throughout Europe, remained a secret until the opening of the Vienna archives in 1919. It is now known that the alliance of Germany, Austria, and Italy was a steadying force in Central Europe, for it suspended, if it did not eliminate, the operation of at least one lively cause of war, namely the competition between Austria and Italy for Trent, Istria, and the eastern coast of the Adriatic. The general aim of the Triple

Alliance Powers was stated in the preamble of the Treaty of the 20th May 1882 to be

> to increase the guaranties of the general peace, to fortify the monarchical principle and thereby to assure the unimpaired maintenance of the social and political order in their respective States.

As the text of the Treaty was secret (and the secret was most successfully preserved), there is no reason to suppose that the wording of the preamble was disingenuous. That the *Triplice* could not become an engine of offensive warfare is clear from Article III :

> If one or two of the High Contracting Parties without direct provocation on their part, should chance to be attacked and to be engaged in a war with two or more Great Powers non-signatory to the present Treaty, the *casus foederis* will arise simultaneously for all the High Contracting Parties.

The absence of any offensive aim was further emphasized by the Declaration (secret like the rest of the Treaty) attached by Italy to the Treaty, with the consent of the other two allies :

> The Royal Italian Government declares that the provisions of the secret Treaty concluded May 20, 1882, between Italy, Austria-Hungary, and Germany, cannot, as has previously been agreed, in any case be regarded as being directed against England.

Thus the Triple Alliance eliminated chances of war, and went far to justify the claim of Treitschke that the union of Germany gave stability to what had been previously a politically weak and dangerous region between western and eastern Europe. It was a guarantee of two *faits accomplis*—the union of Germany and the union of Italy. Strictly defensive in form, the *Triplice* did also inspire confidence in its members for aggressive designs. Undoubtedly it gave such confidence to Austria in her Balkan designs (for instance, the annexation of Bosnia and Herzegovina in 1908), and to Italy in her invasion of Tripoli in 1911.

The Triple Entente was a group formed with a similar aim within the Concert Powers. Its object was the maintenance of the *status quo*. After 1871 France, without a friend in Europe, felt that she was still exposed to German hostility : her eastern frontier had been weakened, her resources diminished, and her unfriendly neighbour had become infinitely more powerful. She therefore welcomed the advances of Russia, and the alliance of 1894. Meanwhile she was recouping her resources and regaining her self-respect through colonial expansion. Here, however, she clashed with England—in West Africa, in the Sudan, in the fisheries of Newfoundland. Fortunately the statesmen of both Powers saw that the world was large enough for each of them : and by a series of acts in 1904 they removed the causes of friction, by mutual give and take. These compensation acts constitute the Dual Entente of 1904. In 1907 the British and Russian Governments adjusted their differences over Afghanistan and Tibet. Thus Great Britain, France, and Russia were grouped together by diplomatic acts, the object of which was to prevent disturbance of the existing territorial situation in Europe, in Asia, and in Africa.

The interests of the Triple Alliance and of the Triple Entente were the same, although neither group felt that they could trust the other, owing to certain particular disturbing influences, such as the Prussian fear of Russia, and the aims of certain *Junkers* to acquire more power for their country. The Concert was not complete enough to remove these disturbing influences. The existence of the Triple Alliance and Entente within the Concert was a proof of its incompleteness. It was necessary, if European peace was to be preserved, that the Concert should be reorganized on a more complete basis. An opportunity for this was provided by the destruction of the old Concert in the Great War. It was to be replaced by a more organized body, the League of Nations.

§ 3

The war of 1914–18 made a broad chasm across the surface of the European States System which, indeed, practically disappeared, and had to be recast at the Conference of Paris in the first half of the year 1919, and by the Treaty of Versailles on 28th June 1919, and the subsidiary treaties.

This Treaty, surely the most elaborate of the world's diplomatic instruments, has four hundred and forty articles, and was signed by the representatives of twenty-eight States. It is the fourth in the series of acts, which starting with the Peace of Westphalia in 1648 provided through Utrecht, Vienna, and Versailles, a *ratio scripta*, a written System, for Europe. Since the Peace of Westphalia, each great settlement has been built on the one before, thus recognizing such necessary growth and adaptation of the European System as must come with the process of time and the changing of circumstances. On the whole the effect of the first three settlements—Westphalia, Utrecht, Vienna—was conservative. But when the last settlement came to be made, at the Conference of Paris in 1919, such colossal damage had been done to the old System, that complete restoration was impossible. Old landmarks had disappeared; so that the re-established States System, as it appeared in the Treaty of Versailles, was in important respects different from the old. Yet it must be noticed that some of the changes were really bringing back conditions which had existed before the wars of the nineteenth century.

The main changes made or recognized by the Treaty were four. Firstly, the provinces of Alsace and Lorraine, which France had lost in 1870–1, were given back to her. Thus the work of Richelieu and Louis XIV, in making for France a stable eastern frontier, was restored. Secondly, the State of Poland, after more than a hundred years' oblivion, was reconstituted. Thirdly, Bohemia, under the title of Czecho-Slovakia, once more (after

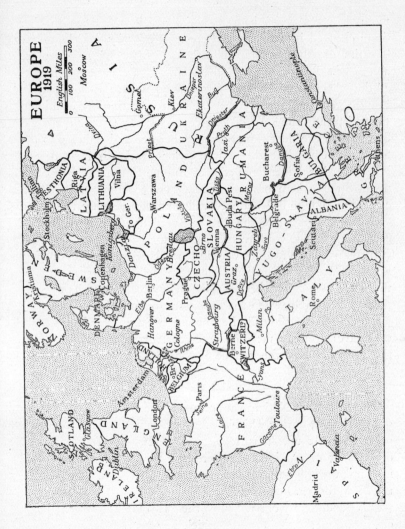

EUROPE
1919

English Miles
0   100   200   300

more than 400 years) became an independent State. Another State changed its international condition, for by Article 31 the Treaties of 1839 guaranteeing the neutrality of Belgium are abrogated. But the greatest change of all—a change which casts all the others into the shade—is the disappearance of the Austrian Empire from the map of Europe. The re-creation of Poland and Bohemia, the filling up of east-central Europe with two solid States, is an excellent thing, giving coherence and stability to the States System. But the disintegration of the Empire of the Habsburgs has left a large area of Europe to a number of competing States, where formerly there was one economic and political control. Time and experience will doubtless remedy this : the ' Succession States ' of the former Austrian Empire are already cementing themselves into the European System.

It was not the Treaty of Versailles which destroyed the Austrian Empire. That State had crumbled to pieces in the last months of the war. The Treaty of Versailles merely recognized its dissolution. Fortunately, when the European System was thus wrecked, for a time at least, until the Succession States should establish themselves firmly, a piece of large constructive statesmanship in the Treaty created the League of Nations.

§ 4

The League of Nations thus comes at the end of a long period of experiment, during which a States System has been in process of being built up, in spite of many failures, cataclysms, and disasters of every kind. It represents the permanent effort of mankind towards international law and order, and at the same time towards national freedom.

It is the difficulty of reconciling these two things—international order and national freedom—which has prevented the rise of world empires since the fall of Rome. Mankind will not tolerate an empire of the world, no more than Europe will tolerate an empire of Europe. Individual States prefer to remain individual—sometimes larger, sometimes smaller, but still separate and individual. So that in modern times Europe came no nearer to being a real States System except as possessing a more or less lively consciousness of membership of a group of States with common civilization and ideals (such consciousness as existed from 1648 to 1815), or of a somewhat closer but still loose Concert, with a common diplomatic practice, such as existed from 1815 to 1914. The League of Nations comes as something more definite, more organized, not purely occasional and voluntary like the Concert, but permanently functioning and with some such amount of compulsory power as is compatible with national freedom : and, moreover, with its membership not limited to Europe but drawn from the States of the world.

The war of 1914 arose owing to the imperfection of the Concert. The habit of it was not sufficiently engrained in the statesmen and politicians of Europe to ensure that the differences of Austria and Serbia should be submitted to arbitration ; nor was confidence in it sufficiently strong to take away from the Germans their fear of Russia ; nor yet was respect for the Concert deep enough to prevent a large part of the Prussian Junker class, who seemed still to be living as if in the days of Frederick the Great, from dreaming of a European Empire. The murders at Sarajevo, the Austrian ultimatum to Serbia, the Russian mobilization, and the German invasion of Belgium came in one swift series, while Europe had no organization in being which could deal with the crisis in the brief time before the flood of warfare broke the dams of peace.

Once the great war had started, each State was thrown back upon its own resources and had to fight for mere existence ; and it was the duty of every statesman to try and make his country win the war. Fortunately, the side which had from the first proclaimed its belief in the Public Law which war was sweeping away, gained the victory ; and even before the war ended plans for a new and more adequate States System had been sketched out and considered by the statesmen of the Entente Powers and America. The scheme ultimately adopted was substantially that which General Smuts had drawn up and which was circulated as a War Cabinet Memorandum in the first half of the year 1918. It was further put into form by a Committee, in which President Wilson, Léon Bourgeois, Lord Robert Cecil, and General Smuts were the moving personages, at the Conference of Paris in the spring of 1919. Now, under the name of the Covenant of the League of Nations, it occupies Part I of the Treaty of Versailles of the 28th June 1919.

The League of Nations had many precursors in the world of thought—the Grand Design of Henri-Quatre (1610), the Project of Everlasting Peace of the Abbé de Saint-Pierre (1714), and Kant's Essay on Perpetual Peace (1795). The Holy Alliance of 1815 was an attempt to put thought into practice. But all projects for everlasting peace failed largely because no State would trust any inter-State organization with the vast amount of power necessary to enforce such peace. The Concert of Europe, on the other hand, failed because it had no compelling force at all. The League of Nations offers a reasonable compromise between the sacrifice of independence on the part of the constituent States, on the one hand, and the wielding of universal despotic dominion on the other.

The League is a purely voluntary association. Any State is free to apply for admission. Admission is granted by a vote of two-thirds of the Assembly. The organs of the League are the Secretariat, which is a permanent body of officials, and a Council and Assembly. The Council consists of Representatives of the ' Principal Allied and Associated Powers ' who figured in the Conference of Paris, together with Representatives of four other Members of the League. The Assembly consists of representatives of every Member. The chief aim and method of the League are contained in Articles 10 to 18 of the Covenant :

The Members of the League undertake to respect and preserve as against external aggression the territorial integrity and political independence of all Members of the League. . . . (Art. 10.)

The Members of the League agree that if there should arise between them any dispute likely to lead to a rupture, they will submit the matter either to arbitration or to inquiry by the Council, and they agree in no case to resort to war until three months after the award by the arbitrators or the report by the Council. (Art. 12.)

The Council shall formulate and submit to the Members of the League for adoption plans for the establishment of a Permanent Court of International Justice. (Art. 14.)

Every treaty or international engagement entered into hereafter by any Member of the League shall be forthwith registered with the Secretariat and shall as soon as possible be published by it. No such treaty or international engagement shall be binding until so registered. (Art. 18.)

The programme thus outlined in the Covenant was ambitious, but it was not expected to bear perfect fruit all at once. The Council of the League has pursued its aims modestly; it has not attempted too much. And yet there is reason to believe that the League has already found solutions or partial solutions for crises which would otherwise have made four wars. These crises were concerned with the Åland Islands (between Sweden and Finland), with Vilna (between Poland and Russia: here the League's solution was not accepted by the interested parties, yet it staved off hostilities for the time being), with Upper Silesia (between Poland and Germany), and with Albania (in a misunderstanding between that country and Serbia in the spring of 1922).

The Court of International Justice sits at the Hague. The rest of the League offices are at Geneva; and the annual meetings of the Assembly in September, and most committee meetings, are open to the public. Until Germany and the United States join it, the League cannot exercise its full weight in international affairs. Still, it is potent for good in many ways: its meetings and its reports create public opinion in favour of International Law ; its active officials and representatives study the difficult questions of the day and offer skilful solutions ; and through its Mandates Section it stands for justice towards all races who, unable to administer themselves, are governed by a stronger Power. Side by side with the League each State of the world manages its own affairs, has its own defensive organization, and its own diplomacy. The daily intercourse of States must always be conducted through State channels—the Foreign Offices and the Chancelleries, the State Departments, as they are variously called. The Great Powers can still meet in Conference, as the Supreme Council of the chief ministers of Great Britain, France, Italy, Belgium, and Japan meet, to liquidate the affairs of the Great War and to execute the Treaty of Versailles.

Thus the continuity of European life has been maintained. The War has passed over the face of the world, and obliterated many landmarks. The Habsburg Empire has disappeared, and the ' Succession States ' of Czecho-Slovakia, Hungary, the kingdom of the Serbs, Croats and Slovenes, and Greater Rumania, have taken its place, along with the land-locked Republic of Austria.

There is still a European System, but Russia is outside it, and Central Europe, though inside it, cannot speak with one voice : it is, for the moment, almost like a political Tower of Babel. Actually, when the European System has at last acquired a Constitution, and when the greatest Asiatic States have come into partnership with it, the private antagonisms of its members seem as acute as ever before. Yet every crisis proves, by the tremors which agitate all seats of government, that the States of the whole world are like Dante's *Monarchia* both *one* as well as *many*. The System is no longer merely European : it is world wide. Yet its centre is in Europe, for this old continent has political traditions unbroken from the past, from the Empire of Augustus and the mild over-lordship of the Antonines.